Natural Healing for

Dogs

and

Cats

a-z

Cheryl Schwartz, D.V.M.

Hay House, Inc.
Carlsbad, California • Sydney, Australia
Canada • Hong Kong • United Kingdom

Published and distributed in the United States by:
Hay House, Inc., P.O. Box 5100, Carlsbad, CA 92018-5100 • (800) 654-5126 • (800) 650-5115 (fax)

Editorial: Jill Kramer • Cover and Interior Design: Christy Salinas
Illustrations: Sarajo Frieden

The author of this book does not dispense medical advice or prescribe the use of any technique as a form of treatment for physical or medical problems without the advice of a veterinarian, either directly or indirectly. The intent of the author is only to offer information of a general nature to help in the quest for your pet's physical and emotional well-being. In the event you use any of the information in this book for your pet, which is your constitutional right, the author and the publisher assume no responsibility for your actions.

Library of Congress Cataloging-in-Publication Data

Schwartz, Cheryl (Cheryl M.)
      Natural healing for dogs and cats A-Z / Cheryl Schwartz.
          p. cm.
      Includes bibliographical references (p.).
      ISBN 1-56170-666-3 • ISBN 1-56170-793-7 (tradepaper)
        1. Dogs–Diseases–Alternative treatment–Handbooks, manuals, etc.
        2. Cats–Diseases–Alternative treatment–Handbooks, manuals, etc. 3. Holistic veterinary
medicine–Handbooks, manuals, etc. I. Title.

SF991 .S3235 2000
636.7'08955–dc21   99-045845

ISBN 1-56170-793-7

05 04 03 02   5 4 3 2
1st printing, March 2000
2nd printing, August 2002

Printed in China by Palace Press

Contents

APPENDIX

Introduction

Healing the Whole Way

After more than 20 years of practicing natural and holistic veterinary medicine with cats and dogs, I have come to realize that it is the most gentle and effective approach to return your animals to health and keep them there.

Although I was trained as a regular veterinarian, I found Western medicine's approach narrow and heavy-handed. I could fix *parts* of the animal, but no one ever mentioned "whole-being wellness"—restoring balance on the physical, behavioral, and mental levels and making the animal happy and healthy.

Now, with holistic and natural healing techniques gaining a stronger foothold in the veterinary community, more than 2,500 veterinarians are practicing natural forms of energy medicine. Using modalities such as acupuncture, massage, chiropractic, herbs, homeopathy, flower essences, and nutrition, we are coping with chronic and acute problems that are plaguing the animal population.

As cats and dogs live with us for longer periods of time, they are privy to our habits and faults, facing environmental toxins, antibiotic overuse, commercial convenience foods, and chemical parasite products. As a result, they are developing more complex imbalances affecting the immune system. They also get stomach ulcers, inflammatory bowel disease, high cholesterol, and thyroid and heart disorders. In short, they mirror *all* of our problems.

You, the public, are seeking more natural forms of healing for yourselves, and when you respond well to them, you want similar care for your animal friends. It's true that natural healing requires more time and energy, but I assure you that healing in a holistic way gives you and your animal friend the opportunity to work together toward a happy future.

The Wave of the Future—Integrative Veterinary Medicine

Acupuncture, herbs, or homeopathy can work hand-in-hand with Western medicine, or entirely on their own. As you will see from the conditions discussed in this book, many approaches exist that will treat common and chronic problems. Natural methods help those animals who are sensitive to Western medication, or in those vague or complex circumstances where there is no actual diagnosis. Although blood tests, ultrasounds, x-rays and Western drugs may still be utilized, true healing requires redirecting or fortifying the animal's energy. Acupuncture, herbs, diet, and homeopathy fill this bill.

Acupuncture and Acupressure

Acupuncture utilizes the body's own energy to heal itself. Professional practitioners place very thin sterile needles into *acupuncture* points that pierce the skin to connect with a flow of energy called *Qi* (also known as *chi*). The energy is directed toward an internal organ system to strengthen it, or through muscle circulation to relieve pain.

Acupressure uses *finger pressure* in these same acupoints on the body's surface to yield similar effects. Professionals train for years to master this scientific art, yet I have seen that the close bond formed between you and your animal friend can facilitate the effectiveness of acupressure, even without years of study. Your intention to help your animal, coupled with your animal's receptivity to your touch, yields the most rewarding and surprising results. So don't hesitate to try it.

When you do acupressure, relax first, breathe easily, and take a moment to clear your mind. Most people use their index finger. Don't bend it, but use a straight-fingered approach. Apply steady, even pressure, not too hard or too soft. Let the animal tell you how much pressure is necessary. Press or *hold* a point for 30 to 60 seconds at a time, and then move to the next point.

Massage in general will relax your pet, relieve muscle tension, and open the flow of energy and circulation. There are numerous massage techniques, such as long strokes, small circular motions, or sweeps using the palms of your hand. Experiment with what your pet likes. After all, part of the human-animal bond involves petting. We love doing it, and they love getting it.

How Do I Use Herbs with My Animal Friends?

Herbs are medicines that come from plants. Plants bring with them their life experiences and help heal by their medicinal virtues as well as their vitality. Herbs

have been used by every culture since the beginning of time to heal the body, mind, and spirit. Some of the plants listed in this book are so common that they may actually grow in your garden. So, before pulling your weeds, consult these pages to see if you might need them.

If they are not in your garden, the herbs listed in this book are readily available in health food stores, or in Chinese pharmacies if you happen to be living near one. Most herbs sold in health food stores at this time are ethically grown and effective. I suggest you establish a relationship with your health food store salesperson to find out the most popular brands.

The dosages I have listed here come from experience over the last 20 years. As any animal may be *allergic* to any substance, including herbs, you might watch for any unsolicited reaction. For the most part, if an herb doesn't agree with the animals, vomiting, diarrhea, appetite, or energy loss may occur. If this happens, stop the herb, and the effects should leave within a day.

Listed here are dried herbs that can be mixed directly with foods or made into teas known as *infusions* or *decoctions*. When tinctures are indicated, they are diluted with distilled or spring water, as tinctures are made from alcohol and will burn your animal's stomach. So please don't use them undiluted. Sometimes the herbs will come in capsules or tablets. The dosage indicated is based on the weight of your animal. Those who are weaker, or more sensitive, may require a lower dose at first, working up slowly to avoid any side effects.

What Is Homeopathy?

Homeopathy uses minute amounts of plant, mineral, or animal substances found in nature. These are diluted with water and shaken, or *succussed,* hundreds to thousands of times. During the process of dilution and succussion, energy molecules are released into the solution, which activate its healing function. It is this activated energy that stimulates your animal's response.

The science of homeopathy is based upon the premise that like cures like—that is, that some natural substances exist in a crude form that can create the same type of symptoms an individual or animal is experiencing. When given a diluted, activated form of this natural substance, patients respond by redirecting and rebalancing their internal energies to return to health.

The diluted preparations are called *remedies,* which were initially taken by healthy volunteers. These individuals then reported the physical, emotional, and mental symptoms they experienced to homeopathic physicians who accumulated these findings. It was found that the more diluted the remedy was—that is, the more it was shaken and the more energy particles released—the stronger the remedy became, and the more profound its results. After enough volunteers reported their findings, books were compiled listing these symptoms and corresponding *remedy pictures.*

Thus, the science of homeopathy is based upon patient symptoms rather than the name of a disease. Homeopathy understands that illness and symptoms are the

individual's (or animal's) attempt to restore itself to health. The homeopathic physician/veterinarian seeks to match the individual/animal with a specific remedy picture.

Books that list physical, emotional, and mental symptoms with groups of homeopathic remedies that might be of assistance in balancing out an individual's/animal's problems are called *repertories*. So, to use a repertory, you need to know the symptoms. Books that list entire symptom pictures of specific remedies are called *materia medicas*. So, to use a materia medica, you need to know the name of a remedy and the personality of your patient.

For example, someone has arthritis in the elbow. You look up "elbow" in the repertory. Under "elbow" you see different types of disorders. You look at "elbow, pain." In this section, several types of pain are listed, including pains that worsen with motion, while lying still, upon rising, at specific times of the day, or during cold or damp weather.

A number of remedies are listed, and then you need to look in the materia medica and match the type of individual or animal you are treating with one of these remedies. The materia medica will tell you the mental state of the individual who requires this remedy—irritable, sad, timid, and so on, and possibly some other physical symptoms the person may be exhibiting.

Professional homeopathic practitioners study these remedy pictures and are adept at matching a specific remedy to a specific patient. As homeopathy is based upon the *totality* of the symptoms—mental and physical—that an individual or animal is showing, a deep healing can occur when the two meet. This is known as *constitutional prescribing* and is what yields the finest results.

The homeopathic remedies listed in this book are meant to treat acute situations, to relieve discomfort, and may not be constitutional. I have used these in my practice and find them to be effective means of treatment.

Dosage in homeopathy is exactly opposite to what we understand in Western medicine. Giving less is better. So give the remedies as indicated, and re-dose *only* when your animal seems to need them again.

Healing by Flower—Using the Essences

Flowers bring joy to our senses. The smell of a rose can bring about healing at the most primitive level. The softness of a petal is indescribable. And, the colors of wildflowers can delight our eyes and our heart.

Flower essences are homeopathic dilutions of flowers. The flowers are set in water in direct sunlight and left to stand. Later, the *essence* released into the water is diluted in brandy and bottled in small dark glass bottles to protect them from further response. The flower essences carry with them emotional stabilizers. We can use them to help balance out fear, worry, depression, or anger.

A flower essence enables its user to feel the emotion and to work through it. This ability of feeling without numbness or panic makes it unique, as tranquilizers and antidepressants merely subdue our views without necessarily working things out.

Flower essences can be added to your animal's water bowl or mixed into a 1-ounce dropper bottle filled with distilled water. The diluted essence can also be rubbed into the ear flaps, on the paw pads, or sprayed from an atomizer into the room. Always stir or shake the bottle against your hand to activate the essence.

Diet

Foods can act as an extension of herbal therapy. In Chinese medicine, each food has a specific association with an organ, a certain inherent temperature, or ability to move energy and blood in a specific direction.

Every one of you who has bitten into a red hot chile pepper knows that it is *hot*. It burns your mouth. It makes your head sweat. It burns on the other end when it comes out the next day. In food therapy, red chile pepper has an affinity with the heart and lungs and improves circulation. Chile warms the body up and promotes an upward and outward sensation that makes your head perspire. So, chiles can be useful at the onset of a nose or head cold (where your head begins to feel congested), and it opens the pores to ease the congestion, allowing the virus to be "sweated out." Chiles are also useful in moderation for stimulating sluggish circulation.

The diet recommendations listed are based on Chinese food therapy and can be used to help bring the body and spirit back into balance.

How to Use This Book

The easiest way to use this book is to look up the condition in the A–Z list. After each listing and brief explanation of the problem, there will be an herb, homeopathic remedy, nutritional supplement, diet recommendation, or acupressure point. I have listed the herbs and certain other remedies in **bold** so you can see at a glance which ones may be needed.

Please remember that this book is to be used as a *guide* only. Use common sense in deciding when to take your animal to the veterinarian. If there is ever a question in your mind, opt for professional consultation. The treatments listed here can always be added to your veterinarian's regimen.

❖❖❖ ❖❖❖

The A–Z List

ABSCESS

An abscess is a pocket of pus and blood that may develop after your pets have been in a fight or have received any type of puncture wound. Claws, teeth, foxtails, splinters, or thorns pierce the skin, making a tiny hole. Bacteria are introduced to the area, and then the skin heals over too quickly. Infection and inflammation flourish, and, voilà—an abscess appears.

With all the fur, you may not even know that your cats and dogs have been fighting or that an abscess is forming. Yet, all of a sudden, they won't eat. They will be lethargic, hot from fever, and reluctant to be touched. If you happen to touch the area, you might elicit a growl or bite.

To treat an abscess:

— *Calm the animal:* Give **Bach Flower Rescue Remedy**, diluted 15 drops to 1 ounce of spring water. Use 1–3 teaspoons by mouth, or rub the diluted mix on the ear flaps or paw pads.

— *Clip the fur* carefully around the area.

— *Compress or soak:* To open a draining tract or to keep it open while the healing occurs, apply a tea prepared from **Plantain,** using 1 teaspoon to 1 cup boiling water, steeped 15 minutes and cooled to room temperature. Or, use an **Epsom salt**

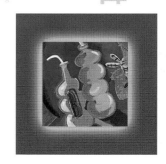

soak, mixing 1 tablespoon salt to 1 cup hot water, and cool. Compress or soak the area 3 times daily for up to 5 minutes per session.

— *Homeopathy:* Home treatment is advisable unless the abscess is in the head area, where the increased blood supply may intensify the infection, causing seizures or other central nervous system signs. Bring your animal to a veterinarian for assistance with abscesses on the head.

To help open the swollen inflamed area, **Belladonna**, at the 30th potency, 4 times daily for 2 days, can be used.

If the abscess is opened and draining slightly with "cheesy," foul-smelling pus, use **Hepar sulphuris** at the 30th potency, 3 times daily for 2–5 days.

If there is thinner, slightly bloody fluid being expelled, use **Silica** at the 12th potency, 3 times daily for 2–5 days.

ANAL GLANDS

Anyone who lives with a dog or cat for any extended period of time knows the peculiar, sometimes foul odor of anal glands. Its pungent fragrance can be left on your pants after your animal friend has visited your lap or during stressful situations such as veterinary visits. Anal glands are located under the tail just inside the anal opening at the level of 5:00 and 7:00.

Being part of the digestive tract, anal glands are supposed to drain regularly when bowel movements pass through. If the stool is too thin or the wrong consistency, the anals may not open and drain. An impaction develops, and your animals scoot on their butts, along the rug or grass, frantically trying to open the duct.

If there is constant inflammation in this area, the anal glands may stay open too long, and the animal will "leak" pungent fluid, making the under-tail area moist, stained, or smelly.

Impaction: If you look under the tail, you might see swelling at the anal gland areas of 5:00 and 7:00, or you might just see the crazy scooting.

— *Herbs and compress:* Make a tea infusion of $1/2$ teaspoon **Nettles** and $1/4$ teaspoon each of **Oregon grape root** and **Chamomile flowers,** in 1 cup of boiled water. Steep for 20 minutes, strain and cool, using this mixture as a warm compress over the anal opening. From the outside of the anus, gently squeeze both sides at the level of 5:00 and 7:00 to open the glands.

Leakage: When the anal glands are inflamed, they leak blood- or brown-tinged pungent fluid. Your animal will undoubtedly be licking the area obsessively.

— *Herbs and compress:* Make a tea infusion of $1/4$ teaspoon **Yarrow** or **Horse chestnut** in $1/2$ cup boiled water. Steep for 20 minutes, strain, cool, and apply the solution as a compress several times daily for 3–5 days.

— *Diet:* Because healthy digestion encourages healthy anal glands, add fiber, such as well-cooked brown rice or Psyllium husks, to the diet. Acidophilus combinations, at $1/2–1/3$ the human recommended dosage, also promote healthy gut flora.

ANEMIA AND BLEEDING PROBLEMS

A low red blood cell count or bleeding problems can result from a variety of causes and should be monitored by your veterinarian. You can assist your animals' blood-building by assuring proper absorption of protein, vitamins, and minerals. Adding pancreatic enzymes to the diet that you can obtain at health food stores or through animal product catalogs assists in digestion. Use $1/4$–$1/2$ the recommended human dose, or follow the directions for animal products. Also, add small amounts of beef liver or lean beef, 3 times weekly, along with $1/4$ cup of leafy green vegetables such as kale, and $1/2$ teaspoon of seaweed.

— *Nutritional:* B vitamins supply building blocks for blood cells. Use a multiple synthetic B vitamin, giving $1/2$ a child's dosage, or use $1/2$ teaspoon molasses in the food. Vitamin C, as sodium ascorbate, 250 mg–1,000 mg twice daily, will strengthen blood cell walls so that they will not break down as easily.

— *Herbs:* **Nettles** and **Siberian ginseng** at $1/8$–$1/2$ teaspoon each daily is good for anemia, while **Horse chestnut** tincture, mixed at 9 drops to $1/2$-ounce water, giving $1/2$–2 teaspoons, is helpful for leaky-type hemorrhaging that can occur with autoimmune hemolytic anemia.

APPETITE

Too little appetite: Your animal comes to the food bowl, sniffs, and walks away. You are at your wit's end to inspire healthful eating habits. Either your veterinarian cannot find anything wrong, or this may be the beginning of kidney, liver, or pancreas problems.

In Chinese medicine, too little appetite is considered a vital energy or *Qi* disorder and can be addressed by strengthening the stomach and pancreas.

— *Acupressure:* A point located on the midline of the belly, halfway between the belly button (which looks like a slight skin discoloration or circular depression) and the breastbone can stimulate appetite. Apply light finger pressure here, or massage in a circular direction for 1 minute before mealtime.

— *Herbs:* **Wood betony** stimulates the digestion and decreases nausea. Mix 9 drops of the tincture to 1 ounce distilled or spring water, using $1/2$–1 teaspoon twice daily.

— *Homeopathy:* **Nux vomica** at the 6th potency given once daily for up to 3 days stimulates the appetite—especially for cats or dogs who have pushy personalities or irritability if they don't get their way.

Sulphur, at the 6th or 12th potency, given as a single dose, applies to the cat or dog who will come to the bowl appearing hungry, and then sniff or look at the food and walk away. These animals will tend to be thirsty for long drinks. The cats who respond to sulphur are usually very vocal and may wake you up at 5:00 A.M. for food, just to snub it and walk away from the bowl.

Too big of an appetite: Your animals are crazy for food and will literally eat anything that is not nailed down, including furniture, sweaters, dirt, rocks, or cat litter. I believe they are eating to get rid of the burning in their stomach.

This might be a symptom of a thyroid, heart, or stomach ulcer disorder and should be checked by your veterinarian. You might change the diet or add herbs or homeopathy.

— *Diet:* The most important thing is to change the diet by adding cooling or moistening foods a la Chinese food therapy. Mashed kidney beans or peas, tofu, millet, barley, buckwheat, celery, and string beans curb inflammation. Minimizing red meat-, chicken-, or shrimp-based commercial pet food is advisable, substituting cod, sole, or other light fish as the protein source.

— *Herbs:* **Calendula** flower tea using 1 teaspoon dried herb to 1 cup boiled water helps cool stomach inflammation. Steep for 15 minutes and strain, using 1/2 teaspoon to 2 tablespoons tea 15 minutes before a meal, and then between meals if the animal seems to be burping or looking uncomfortable.

— *Homeopathy:* **Hydrastis canadensis** mother tincture, mixed at 9 drops to 1 ounce distilled water, and using 1/2–1 teaspoon before meals, helps the animal who eats everything, then vomits it back up. The animal may drool thick saliva frequently and be sensitive to your touching its abdomen. They may also groom their bellies excessively to assuage the discomfort.

ARTHRITIS

This condition can affect the young or old, making the joints ache and the back or limbs sore. Some problems are worse in damp, cold conditions; at the onset of storms; or when the weather abruptly changes.

— *Acupressure and massage:* In Chinese medicine, it is believed that pain results from a blockage of energy or blood circulation to a specific area. So, keeping the flow happening can relieve pain.

A gentle massage on either side of the spine in a downward circular direction can increase circulation. Your animal will show you how much pressure is necessary.

There is an acupressure point, located in the "hollow" just in front of the outside of the hind leg ankle (in front of the Achilles tendon), where you can press lightly for 15 seconds at a time to alleviate pain.

— *Nutritional:* **Vitamin E** given once daily at 50 IU for small dogs or cats, up to 400 IU for large dogs, plus 20–50 mcg. **Selenium** acts as a good anti-inflammatory agent. Caution should be used if high blood pressure exists.

Antioxidant combinations with **Glucosamine** and **Chondroitin Sulphate** at 250–1,000 mg daily helps maintain smooth joint surfaces.

— *Herbs:* **Nettles** or **Alfalfa** at 100 mg–500 mg daily mixed with food helps with joint circulation and pain.

— *Homeopathy:* A remedy can be given 1–2 times daily for 1–3 days. Relief should be apparent during this time—if it is the correct remedy. Remedies of the 6th, 12th, or 30th potency may be used, with a dose being 1 pellet for a small dog or cat, to 3 pellets for a large dog. Repeat a remedy if it has been effective during the next episode of discomfort.

Rhus toxidendron is helpful for arthritis that is worse when animals first start to move, but then "warm" out of it as they continue moving, getting painful again after too much action. These animals will feel worse during wet, cold weather or when the weather abruptly changes. They also tend to have diarrhea episodes with blood, or panting or breathing problems at night.

Ruta graveolens can be used for arthritis of the elbow, wrist, or ankle joint where there is little muscle but a lot of tendon or ligament attachments.

Bryonia alba is beneficial for animals who feel pain with any kind of motion. They also like to lie on the side that hurts them because pressure makes it feel better. This animal prefers cool, cloudy days.

Calcarea carbonica helps animals that are slightly overweight, sensitive to food changes, and who have had bone problems from a young age. Golden Retrievers seem to do well with this remedy. The arthritis is worse in wet, cold weather, and the animal seems to have a numbness over the affected leg that reveals itself as stumbling or collapse when they arise.

BAD BREATH

Puppy kisses or cat baths can reveal less-than-kissing-sweet breath. Regular teeth cleaning by your veterinarian can help. In between cleanings, use raw beef knuckle bones with some meat on them to help clean teeth and to stimulate good gastric juices. Bad breath can well up from the stomach or lungs, as well as from the teeth and gums. So, notice any peculiar breathing or gurgling problems.

— _Nutritional:_ Use chlorophyll to sweeten the breath, correct stomach pH, and stimulate the flow of gastric juices. Adding a pinch of basil, oregano, or dill to food enhances digestion.

— _Supplements:_ Give $\frac{1}{4}$ to 1 teaspoon of liquid chlorophyll to the animal.

BARKING EXCESSIVELY

This occurs when your dog desires attention, either for physical or emotional reasons. Many working breeds, such as cattle dogs, have been bred to do a job. They actually _need_ an occupation, and may resort to barking if they don't get one.

— _To treat excessive barking,_ see if the animal requires physical attention; investigate using massage techniques.

— _Massage_ along both sides of the neck, backbone, and legs to test for discomfort. If there is sensitivity, your dog may need to be seen by a veterinarian. If no sensitivity is found, emotional disturbance may be a large part of the problem. In this case, _assure_ your animal by sliding the palm of your hand under the chest between the front legs. Hold your hand there for 1 or 2 minutes to calm your animal.

— _Nutritional:_ Barking and agitation may intensify from digestive tract or other inflammation, which decreases the amount of fluids that nourish the cells. Adding a handful of foods such as lettuce, celery, cucumbers, pickles, or blueberries to the diet can bring added moisture and cooling to the body and spirit.

— _Flower essences_ from the Bach Flower Society or Flower Essence Society of California help treat emotional imbalances. For agitation and barking, use 3 drops each of **Aspen, Vervain,** and **Heather** essences to a half-pint water bowl.

BITE WOUNDS

Sometimes bite wounds can be detected once you see that your animal is limping or bleeding. Other times, bite wounds are subtle, marked by a wet or matted fur area, a look of triumph or horror, or a reluctance to go outside again. If bite wounds are not treated early on, they may develop abscesses.

— _To treat bite wounds,_ separate the hair carefully to expose the puncture. Gently clip the fur and wash the area with a diluted mixture of **Calendula flower** tea mixed with ¼ teaspoon of **Hypericum** (St. John's wort) tincture to dull the pain. Hydrogen peroxide is always a good standby to use when cleansing the area (but it stings).

— _Homeopathy:_ **Ledum palustre** and **Arnica montana** at the 30th potency can be given 3 times during the first hour following the bite, or as close thereafter as possible. Repeat the remedies once later that day or the next.

If the area is very bruised, Arnica can be repeated 3 times daily for the next 3 days. Arnica topical sprays are also available if you can work them through the fur.

BRONCHITIS

Acute bronchitis from infection should be monitored by your veterinarian, as these infections can be life threatening. In addition to Western treatment, or in cases of "allergic bronchitis," acupressure and herbs along with nutritional supplements may help your animal.

— *Acupressure:* Massage along the crease made in the elbow from inside to outside when you flex the front leg, and on the back between the shoulder blades.

— *Herbs:* Mix equal parts of dried crushed **Elecampane + Wild cherry bark + Marshmallow root**. Use $1/16$–$1/2$ teaspoon of the mix with some food, or fill capsules, twice daily, depending on the size of the animal.

— *Nutritional:* **Vitamin C** at 125–500 mg twice daily works as a natural bronchodilator. **Vitamin E** and **Evening primrose oil** decrease inflammation in the respiratory tract. Use 50 IU–400 IU. Cod liver oil, using $1/4$–1 teaspoon daily, nourishes the cilia lining the windpipe.

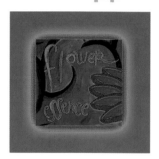

BURNS

Animals may burn their paw pads from walking on severely hot surfaces,. Or, they may burn their skin from getting too close to heating sources or from excessive sunlight, if they are white.

— *Topical applications:* **Aloe vera gel**, **Panthenol** (a precursor of vitamin B_5), or **Egg white** will take pain away and help heal skin. **Calendula** ointment soothes and heals burnt paw pads and ear flaps.

Natural sunscreens applied to the ears of light-colored cats help protect against sunburn. Obviously, keeping them out of the sun during peak heat times of the day is advisable.

— _Herbs:_ Internally, **Nettles** and **Alfalfa** at $1/8$–$1/2$ teaspoon twice daily will regenerate tissue.

BURPING

Although occasional burps may be normal, especially if your animal eats fast, there may be an imbalance if burping occurs frequently. It is highly unusual for cats to burp.

— _Massage:_ Rub the belly in a downward direction on the midline, especially between the breastbone and the belly button.

— _Herbs:_ Make a tea with a pinch of **Cardamom seeds**, and $1/8$ teaspoon each of **Dill** and **Papaya leaf** in one cup of boiling water, steeping 10 minutes, straining, cooling, and giving 1–2 tablespoons, 10 minutes prior to eating.

CANCER

Once cancer has been diagnosed, the body has been in a struggle for a long time, even if you did not see signs. Cancer arises when the body's vital force can no longer compensate for the confusion taking place throughout the immune system.

Homeopathy may be helpful, with specific constitutional remedies prescribed for each animal by a trained practitioner.

Herbal research in Japan has shown many varieties of mushrooms to be helpful in decreasing the spread of cancer. Species such as **Ganoderma lucidum, Japonicum,** and **Tremella** contain polysaccharides that inhibit production of new cancer cells.

Chinese tonic herbs for general vitality, or Qi, such as **Astragalus, Codonopsis, Siberian ginseng,** and **Schizandra,** along with blood tonics such as **Tang kuei** and **Rehmannia** can stimulate appetite and boost energy for the animal even after chemotherapy has been administered. Many of these supplements are available through health food stores and are distributed through American and European companies.

Chinese herbal combinations also include antimicrobial substances and ingredients that direct the energy in the body and help relieve pain.

These are safe for animals and can be given at $1/4$–$2/3$ the human recommended dose depending upon the animal's weight.

— *Nutritional:* Antioxidants that eat up toxic waste in the body, such as **Vitamins C and E,** can strengthen the immune system. Give as much vitamin C as your ani-

mal friend can tolerate without getting diarrhea. Ester forms seem better tolerated. Vitamin E can be added up to 800 IU daily, along with **Co-enzyme Q10** at 10–30 mg daily, to decrease inflammation and increase oxygenation to the normal cells. Small amounts of micro algae such as **Spirulina** supply minerals and food building blocks.

Of course, *the* most important thing is to keep the animal eating, as nausea or pain can interfere with appetite. Dietwise, entice your animal with as many fresh, organic foods as possible, emphasizing hormone-free meats in small amounts for anemia and weight loss problems, and well-cooked cracked grains for feverish animals. Fish such as salmon contain the Omega-3 fatty acids, which are helpful for relieving inflammation.

— *Acupressure:* A point located behind the front ankle, above the secondary pad on the back of the front leg, can be massaged to relieve nausea. Add to this a point located on the inside of the hind paw just in front of the ankle to increase the absorption of foods.

CATARACTS AND SENILE DYSTROPHY OF THE LENS

When you look into the eyes of your animal and see a white, light blue, or opaque disc, chances are they are cataracts, or what is known as "senile dystrophy of the lens."

Cataracts form from a hardening of the lens material so that light does not pass through to the retina, and the animal essentially goes blind. Cataracts can be hereditary, affecting puppies or kittens, or be associated with metabolic diseases such as diabetes.

Senile dystrophy of the lens occurs in older animals as the lens fibers lose their elasticity and coalesce, filtering less light through to the lens. Here, the vision is impaired, especially at night.

— *Homeopathy:* Once cataracts form, it is unlikely that you will be able to reverse them. You may try homeopathic remedies that increase blood and nerve circulation such as **Calcarea phosphorica, Silica,** and **Calcarea fluoride,** all given at the 3rd to 6th potencies, on a rotating daily basis for at least one month, to promote lens clearing.

Senile dystrophy, on the other hand, may be unsightly, but may be helped by nutritional supplements and herbs that encourage nourishment to eye tissue.

— *Nutritional:* Feeding **Unsweetened grape juice** helps to restore fluids to eye tissues. **Cod liver oil,** at $1/2$–1 teaspoon every other day, provides **Vitamin A** for healthy vision. **Vitamin C,** using 100–1,000 mg once daily, **Vitamin B** complex at $1/4$–$1/2$ human dosage, **Zinc** at 5 mg daily, and **Micro algae** in trace amounts, all nourish the eye.

— *Herbs:* Dried **Lycium berries**, available in many health foods stores or in Chinese herbal pharmacies, can be given daily. Use 1–3 berries daily.

Eyebright can be added to food as the dried herb at $1/8$–$1/2$ teaspoon daily, or as a tea to stimulate eye circulation. Eyebright can be used as an eyewash to "brighten" the eyes.

Dried **Rose petals** can be made into a "long infusion" by steeping 1 tablespoon into 1 pint boiling water for 40 minutes, using it strained and cooled as an eyewash. Internally, rose helps increase eye circulation and relieve headaches that may be associated with eye congestion.

CIRCLING AND PACING

Circling and pacing may be signs of internal fever, neurological disorders, or pre-seizure activity. Ear pain or inflammation may also be involved. Please check this out with your veterinarian. Often, however, there is no official cause for the behavior, especially if the animal is a senior. In these cases, I have found diet and acupressure massage to be helpful.

— *Diet:* Avoid foods that can increase internal heat and agitation, such as chicken and shellfish. Instead, substitute protein sources such as fish (cod or sole), and bean products as protein sources. Add string beans, peas, bananas, and lettuce to the diet, as well as $\frac{1}{4}$– $\frac{2}{3}$ teaspoon of kelp powder on a daily basis.

— *Massage* the lower parts of the front legs, especially encircling the front wrists including the secondary paw pad behind the front leg. Rub here several times daily for 1 minute. Also massage the dimples at the back of the head just behind and below the base of the ears.

COAT CONDITION

Some animals have dull or thin hair, implying a problem with blood circulation, food absorption, or general metabolism.

You may need to have your veterinarian check your animal's thyroid gland with a blood test. Also, poor-quality food may contain nutrients but lack the enzymes necessary to make them available to your animal's body. Use commercial foods with chelated, readily absorbable minerals, or add fresh foods to the diet.

— *Nutritional:* Supplements that help make hair strong and glossy include essential fatty acids with Omega 3 and 6 oils such as **Borage** and **Flaxseed.** Give 100–300 mg of either daily. **Vitamin C** at 100–1,000 mg daily helps oxygen and blood reach the skin. **Vitamin E** at 50– 400 IU, plus **Vitamin A** at 5,000–10,000 mg daily (as long as there is no history of liver problems, where A is stored), along with **Biotin** and **Seaweed** for trace minerals, shine and thicken the coat.

COMMON COLD—see *Kennel Cough; Sinus Woes and Sneezing*

COLIC

Your animal may whimper, whine, hide, change position frequently, or sit uncomfortably still when colic pain occurs. Symptoms usually show 15 minutes to $1\frac{1}{2}$ hours after eating. The abdomen will feel tight and hard. If this occurs repeat-

COLIC, cont'd.

edly, you will probably need to change the diet you are feeding, as something is not agreeing with your animal.

— *Massage:* To encourage movement through the digestive tract, gently massage the abdomen in a circular motion from left to right.

— *Herbs:* **Caraway seeds** help relieve gas colic pain. Make a tea infusion using 1 teaspoon crushed seeds to 1 cup boiling water, steep for 15 minutes, strain and cool. Use 1 teaspoon every 15 minutes for 4–6 doses.

— *Homeopathy:* **Colocynthis** in the 6th potency is especially good for the animal who curls up tightly in a ball, sits crunched near the heating vent, or demands hard tummy rubs to relieve the discomfort.

COLITIS

Just as in humans, colitis causes pain and straining when the animal has bowel movements. There may be mucus; blood; or thin, flattened stool.

Severe forms of colitis require veterinary supervision. In addition to conventional treatment, try out a diet change that includes mashed potatoes (use vegetable bouillon for moistening) or mashed turnips, and avoid high fats. Baby cereals made from flakes of oatmeal or rice are well tolerated, as is well-cooked millet.

— *Herbs:* Mix 9 drops each of tinctures of **Plantain + Wild yam + Lady's mantle** into 1 ounce distilled water. Shake the diluted mixture 18 times and use 1–3 teaspoons twice daily. This combination is good for colitis with much mucus or blood.

Do not use if the animal is pregnant, as Wild yam has a strong effect on the uterus.

For pregnant or weak animals, **Slippery elm** helps quiet the intestines. Use ½–1½ teaspoons 3 times daily.

— *Nutritional:* Digestive enzymes and **Lactobacillus** combinations using ¼–½ of the human recommended doses are beneficial to repopulate the good-guy flora in the gut. **Pectin** at ½–1 teaspoon twice daily helps coat the lining of the inflamed intestine and provide fiber.

CONJUNCTIVITIS

You'll know that your animals have conjunctivitis when their eyes become red or itchy and have a nasty discharge streaming from them. The animal may hide from the light or rub the eye on the carpet to show discomfort or frustration. The condition may come on suddenly, or start with redness and progress.

— *Herbs:* A combination of ¹⁄₁₆ teaspoon each of tinctures of fresh **Chickweed + Nettles + Burdock leaf** diluted into 1 pint of boiled water and cooled can be used both internally and as an eyewash to cool the eye down, act as an antiseptic, and moisten inflamed tissues. Internally, give 1–3 teaspoons 4 times daily for up to 1 week.

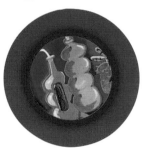

CONSTIPATION

Seeing your cat or dog strain to have a bowel movement, and hearing their cries of pain, frustration, and struggle, can be heartbreaking for any animal lover. Constipation can occur when the body is too dry or when the animal's vitality is too weak to push the stool out. Constipation can also occur if there is a blockage in the intestine that will not allow the stool to pass. If constipation is sudden, please check with your veterinarian. If it is chronic, you may try any of the following remedies.

— _Nutritional:_ Cooked, mashed sweet potatoes or pumpkin help moisten intestines and provide fiber. Flax, psyllium, and sesame seeds provide moistening, while psyllium husk brings high fiber into the diet. One-half to 1½ teaspoons of olive oil help lubricate the intestines.

If your animal is the pushy, aggressive type, feeding it a diet with fish such as cod or sole, plus brown rice, dark green vegetables, and fiber encourages bowel movements. If your animal is timid and very thirsty, on the other hand, feeding a moistening diet that includes tofu, pears, apples, goat milk yogurt, and essential fatty acids is beneficial.

— _Homeopathy:_ **Silica** at the 6th or 12th potency is helpful for sensitive, nervous, and timid animals. They strain a lot to expel the stool, which may get stuck under the tail, coming halfway out and receding again.

— **Alumina** at the 6th potency is helpful for animals with a lot of dandruff, and a slightly irritable or depressed personality. These animals don't seem to have a

desire to pass stool, even if they haven't gone for several days. When there is stool, it is very hard, and blood may come out along with it from irritation.

    — *Herbs:* **Aloe vera juice**, using a #3 capsule for a cat or small dog to a #00 for a large 60-pound dog, once daily. **Swedish bitters**, available in health food stores, with the bitter herb **Gentian,** also helps to regulate bowels. Use a #3–00 capsule once daily.

COUGHING

    Coughs can come from different sources—infections, allergies, chronic inflammation, or more serious conditions involving the lungs or heart. If your animal friends have a chronic cough, please check with your veterinarian.

    — *Herbs:* For dry coughs, **Slippery elm + Elecampane + Wild cherry bark** combinations are useful. Mix together equal parts of each herb, giving $\frac{1}{4}$–$\frac{3}{4}$ teaspoon 3 times daily. Mixing the herbs with a teaspoon of baby food makes them more palatable. Alternately, make a tea of these herbs, adding honey, which will be soothing and possibly easier to administer, using 1 teaspoon to 1 tablespoon 3–4 times daily.

    For moist coughs, mix equal parts of **White horehound + Coltsfoot +** $\frac{1}{2}$ part **Sage.** Combine this with honey to help as an expectorant. Use $\frac{1}{2}$–2 teaspoons up to 4 times daily for 2 weeks.

    — *Homeopathy:* **Spongia toasta** in the 6th to 30th potency 1–3 times daily is

COUGHING, cont'd.

helpful for a croupy, loud cough—like kennel cough—especially when the outer throat area is sensitive to touch. Wheezing and dry asthmatic coughs may also fit into this category.

Antimonium tartaricum in the 6th potency is good for the cough with a lot of mucus and a rattling sound in the chest. Use 3 times daily for up to 1 week.

CYSTITIS (bladder troubles)

There are several common types of cystitis that cats and dogs suffer from—crystal or sand formation with burning or bleeding, straining with frequent trips outside or to the box, and scant urination, which may be bloody because of dehydration.

Recurrent cystitis requires professional assistance. You may add any of the following to the regimen that seems to apply to your animal.

Crystal or sand formation: Your animal urinates and runs around or licks its privates frantically to stop the burning or pain. There are frequent trips to the box, many with normal amounts of shiny urine, reflecting a high number of crystals. This urine may also be blood tinged. The animal is usually thirsty for large amounts of water.

With crystal or sand formation, you need to make sure your animal *is* urinating, as some crystals can block the system, making your animal unable to pass urine.

Not passing urine is a life-threatening situation, and you need to bring the animal to the veterinarian immediately.

— *Herbs:* Tinctures of **Yarrow + Marshmallow root + Plantain,** using 10 drops of each mixed together in 1 ounce of water plus 1 drop of **Gravel root** help decrease inflammation and crystal formation. Give ½–1½ teaspoons 3–4 times daily during acute situations up to 1 week.

Hydrangea helps balance water metabolism in the kidneys, cools the burning sensation, and helps dissipate crystals, especially the uric acid type that Dalmatians produce. Use the tincture at 18 drops dissolved in 1 ounce of distilled water, using ½ teaspoon to 1 tablespoon 2–3 times daily for up to 1 week.

Agrimony, as the flower essence, or tincture, may be added to the drinking water to encourage urine acidity and decrease inflammation. Use 1–5 drops in the water bowl.

For chronic situations, **Cleavers** is very helpful, especially for those kitties who run around frantically after urinating. Cleavers is effective when there are swollen glands in the groin area between the inner thigh and belly.

— *Homeopathy:* **Sepia** in the 15th to 30th potency is helpful especially if there is reddish or sticky sediment that adheres to the fur around the penis or vagina. Emotionally, animals that need Sepia may be annoyed, sad, or sensitive, and physically look almost pear shaped, with a hangy-type belly.

Urtica urens in the 6th potency is helpful if there is much frantic running and licking at the end of urination, indicating burning.

CYSTITIS, cont'd.

Hydrangea in the 6th potency benefits the animal with severe abdominal pain who produces copious amounts of crystals.

Frequent urging and trips to the box: Your cat or dog tries to urinate, but only a small amount comes out. They look miserable and bloated. No blood or crystals are passed that you can see. This animal is not very thirsty, has a gurgly tummy, and usually prefers to be warm.

— *Herbs:* **Lovage root** acts like an herbal diuretic that decongests the bladder area, stimulating urination. Use 9–15 drops of the seed or root tincture in 1 ounce distilled water, giving ½–2 teaspoons 3 times daily for up to 10 days. Caution should be taken with pregnant animals, as Lovage will stimulate uterine contractions and can possibly cause an abortion.

For less severe conditions, **Coriander** seeds and leaves strengthen the urinary tract and promote urination. Use ⅛–¾ teaspoon twice daily in food.

— *Diet:* Avoid wheat products, substituting brown rice in its place. Cranberry concentrate helps to acidify the urine, using ⅓–½ the human recommended dosage, or follow the animal product directions.

Scant urine: Your animal may be getting on in years, and is thirsty but only drinks small amounts at one time. The animal will also tend to be constipated, anxious, and heat sensitive, seeking out the open window or cool cement floors.

— *Herbs:* **Cleavers** cools and moistens the urinary tract, relieving inflammation in the ureter and urethra. Use the freeze-dried or tincture form made from the fresh (not dried) plant to ensure potency. Give $\frac{1}{8}$–$\frac{3}{4}$ teaspoon of the herb twice daily, or dilute 9–15 drops of tincture in 1 ounce of distilled water, using $\frac{1}{2}$–2 teaspoons twice daily.

Alfalfa and **Asparagus** teas also restore fluids to the body.

— _Diet:_ Add barley, sweet potatoes, potatoes, green beans, and cod or sole to the food.

DANDRUFF AND DRY SKIN

Dandruff can be unsightly and also a reflection of poor blood stores or circulation. Use foods and nutritional supplements that bring moisture into the body.

— *Nutrition:* Essential fatty acids can bring out the glow in your animal friend's coat. Sources of fatty acids can be found in fish oils such as cod liver oil, as well as in salmon. Other sources can be found in **Borage** and **Flaxseed** oils. Dosage ranges from $1/2$ teaspoon to 1 tablespoon, depending upon the size of your animal friend.

Trace minerals help with skin metabolism. **Seaweeds, Chlorophyll**, and **Nettles** are loaded with trace minerals to support skin cell growth. Use $1/8$–1 teaspoon daily. Biotin fortifies skin smoothness. Use $1/2$ the human recommended dose.

Sunshine and **Vitamin D,** plus regular exercise, help the exfoliation process and invigorate the circulation.

— *Herbs:* **Polygonum multiflori**, otherwise known as He Shou Wu, is a Chinese patent herbal product available in many health food stores. Its stories about keeping hair black and shiny are folkloric in China. Use 1–3 tablets 1–2 times daily.

Teas made from domestic **Rose** also soften, moisten, and nourish the skin.

— *Massage* all four main paw pads to help stimulate blood circulation.

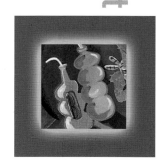

DEMODEX MANGE

Although there are actual mites involved in this condition, the underlying problem is a weakened immune system. Natural healing methods deal primarily with

DEMODEX MANGE, cont'd.

strengthening the immune system, using supplements, fresh foods, herbs, and acupressure.

— *Diet:* Use a complete natural diet with 30% protein, 50% whole grains, and 20% vegetables. Protein can be from whitefish such as cod or sole, or catfish and occasional salmon. Meatwise, hormone-free lean beef or pork, cooked thoroughly in broth with green and yellow vegetables, may be tried. Limit poultry, as this brings more heat into the body according to Chinese food therapy. Up to 2 tablespoons of oil supplements including **Olive, Sunflower, Flax,** or **Safflower** can be given daily, along with the other nutritional supplements listed below.

If you're feeding a commercial diet, make certain it contains only natural preservatives such as **Vitamin E**. Also, add ¼–½ cup fresh grains (cooked with 3 cups of water to 1 cup grain) to bring vital energy into dry or canned food.

— *Nutritional:* **Vitamin C** in the ester form or as sodium ascorbate, given 100–750 mg twice daily, using as high a dose as possible before the onset of diarrhea, fortifies the immune system.

Vitamin E at 50–400 IU once daily is a good antioxidant to clear toxins and relieve inflammation.

Essential fatty acids from **Cod liver oil, Sunflower, Flaxseed,** or **Borage oil**, at 1/4–3 teaspoons once daily, boost immunity.

Trace minerals such as **Seaweeds** or those from **Microalgae** can be used in small amounts, from ¼–⅔ teaspoon daily.

Since dogs with demodex mange have weakened immune systems, they may get diarrhea more easily than others. If this occurs, reduce the supplements and work up gradually.

— *Herbs:* **Dandelion + Burdock roots + Milk thistle seed** combinations help to decongest the liver, improve circulation, and strengthen immunity. Use 250 mg of each daily for 2–3 weeks.

Astragalus strengthens vitality, along with **Siberian ginseng** and **Grape juice,** which assist the adrenal gland. Use 100–200 mg Astragalus, 250 mg Siberian ginseng, and 2 tablespoons natural white grape juice once daily.

— *Acupressure:* Use a point on the front leg located in the web between the dew claw and the paw, rubbing gently for one minute several times daily. (The dew claw is the short thumblike appendage on the inside of the front, and sometimes rear, paws of your animal. Because they are shorter than the other toes, they may suffer injury by getting caught in brush while your animal is running off-trail.)

DIARRHEA

Diarrhea can be infectious, like dysentery from food poisoning. It can also come from parasites or faulty absorption in the body. Dehydration from fluid loss during diarrhea can be serious. Replacement fluid can be given in the form of a children's diarrhea electrolyte solution that is available in supermarkets.

Infectious: In addition to the diarrhea, your cat or dog may be lethargic, running

DIARRHEA, cont'd.

a fever, or refusing food or water.

— *Herbs:* **Plantain,** in tincture form, using 25 drops to 1 ounce distilled water, giving 1–3 droppers full 3–4 times daily for 3 days, curtails diarrhea and acts as an antimicrobial.

Calendula + Yarrow flower tea made by mixing ½ teaspoon Calendula with ⅛ teaspoon Yarrow into 1 cup boiling water, steeped 20 minutes and cooled. Using 1–3 teaspoons daily for up to 1 week helps stop bloody diarrhea and soothe membranes.

Slippery elm soothes and coats sore intestinal membranes. Make a slurry of ¼ teaspoon herb to 1 cup warm water, stir, and give 1–3 teaspoons 3 times daily. When mixed with water, Slippery elm hardens at room temperature. So, use it quickly after making the mixture.

Charcoal tablets help to absorb toxins in the digestive tract. Use 1–3 tablets 3 times daily for 3 days.

— *Homeopathy:* **Podophyllum** in the 6th potency, given 3 times daily for 3 days, will help the dog or cat with lots of gurgles in the stomach, followed by uncontrollable, putrid, sometimes explosive stool. There may be redness and pooching out of the rectum following the stool.

Sulphur fits the picture of the dog or cat who has early-morning diarrhea with a lot of burning or itching around the anus. The cat will cry out and run in anticipation of, or after, the passing of the stool. There may also be a lot of itching that makes the skin red.

Arsenicum album in the 6th to 30th potency is good for animals with diarrhea that may be accompanied by vomiting and severe weakness after the episodes. These animals like to lie down close to heaters or sit in the sun to keep warm. Tainted food may have brought on the symptoms. In general, those animals who benefit from Arsenicum album are the "scaredy cats." They are usually very restless, change position frequently, and are too weak to stand.

— *Diet:* Mashed potatoes or well-cooked millet help stop diarrhea and soothe the intestines. Avoid fatty meats. Small amounts of chicken may be used.

DRY EYE AND PANNUS

When the eye does not receive enough moisture, the tissues on the front of the eye begin to break down, causing redness, irritation, and a mucous discharge. Using the supplements for eye nutrition listed under "Cataracts" are helpful. In addition, massage around the eye, pressing at each corner and at the equivalent of 12:00 and 6:00, stopping 30 seconds in each position.

— *Homeopathy:* If dry eye is caused by frequent blockage of the tear ducts, use Silica in the 6th potency 3 times weekly for up to 1 month to help correct the condition. Animals that benefit from Silica are usually shy and cold, seeking heaters or the sun. They may also suffer from constipation.

If the eyes stay dry, irregular pigment cells can spread across the eye's surface, blocking your animal's vision. This condition is known as *pannus.*

— *Herbs:* In addition to the treatments listed above, bathing the eye in Oatstraw, Dandelion and Chrysanthemum flower tea seems to be helpful. Internally, Lycium berries help nourish the eye. Use 1–3 berries daily.

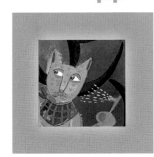

EAR PROBLEMS

Dogs, especially, suffer from a myriad of ear problems. Ears can be too moist, build up wax, or get infected. They can also be invaded by parasites. Chronic ear problems may reflect a deeper problem, so advice from your holistic veterinarian should be sought.

— *Pin up ears:* Some dogs whose ear flaps hang down and cover the ear canals suffer from moist discharges. Sometimes, keeping the ear flaps pinned up with a barrette an hour a day helps.

— *Household products:* Using a few drops of hydrogen peroxide or a mild white vinegar-and-water solution (1 capful to 1 cup of water) to swab out the ears helps to change the pH and introduce oxygen into the ear environment.

— *Herb:* A mild **Plantain** solution may also be used.

— *Ear rubs:* Dogs or cats may develop excessive dark ear wax buildup and shake their heads frequently, demanding ear rubs to move the wax away. Soak a cotton ball with a mixture of 4 parts **Propolyne glycol** (available at drug stores) with 1 part **Calendula** tea or non-alcoholic solution. Add several drops of **Aniseed** oil. Swab the ear canal out with this mixture twice weekly to help break up wax buildup, decrease inflammation, and invigorate the circulation.

Some animals have ear pain accompanied by infections or inflammation. The ear is so sensitive that the animals hide from noise, don't want to be touched, become irritable, or cry out in pain. When you look at the ear, it is red and swollen, and the odor can clear a room. Many of these animals need extensive veterinary care, which includes antibiotics. Unfortunately, although the ear clears up temporarily, the condition returns. Homeopathy seems best suited to these situations, and the best results can be obtained by working with a professional practitioner. At the beginning, you might try any of the following for short-term results.

— *Homeopathy:* **Pulsatilla** at the 12th or 30th potency is especially suited for the animal with acute ear flare-ups with redness, sensitivity to touch, and a yellowish discharge. These animals feel worse when they first come into the house from outside, and they prefer to sit near an open window. These are also the animals who don't like the rain and hate getting their paws wet. Use the remedy 2–3 times daily for several days.

Hepar sulphuris at the 30th potency is useful for the irritable dog or cat who won't let you touch the ears, and who won't even let you get close to the head. The ear is inflamed, and there is a nasty, fetid odor. The discharge can be like yellow cottage cheese. Use 2 doses only, 12 hours apart, in acute situations. Professional guidance may be necessary for continued treatment

Tellurium in the 6th potency given daily for 1 week helps the animal with an odorous discharge that can burn the fur off around and under the ear. The ear is extremely sensitive to touch and discharges a fishlike odor.

Most parasites will succumb to ear preparations containing **Tea tree oil.**

EMERGENCY

On your way to the veterinarian . . .
Bee stings: Use **Apis mel** 10–30c every 15–20 minutes for the first hour.

EMERGENCY, cont'd.

Topically, use **Rescue Remedy** cream, or a diluted spray of 10 drops Rescue Remedy (Bach Flower Essence) to 1 ounce spring water. Alternatively, use a compress of dried **Plantain leaves** wrapped in a gauze pad, and moistened with warm water.

Burns and bites: See listings.

Eye trauma or puncture wounds: Use **Ledum palustre** in the 30th potency every 15 minutes for one hour.

Bleeding, shock, and breathing: Use **Rescue Remedy** diluted 10 drops to $\frac{1}{2}$ ounce spring water, and rub on ear flaps. To stop hemorrhage, **Arnica montana** or **Phosphorus,** at the highest potency available, by mouth; or **Golden thread** root powder sprinkled in wounds. If available in health food stores or Chinese pharmacies, the Vietnamese patent herb **Yunnan pai yao** can be sprinkled on wounds.
— *Acupressure:* A point to stimulate breathing is located on the face, between the nose and upper lip, midway down the crease. Apply fingernail pressure or the tip from a ballpoint pen cap, and stimulate vigorously.

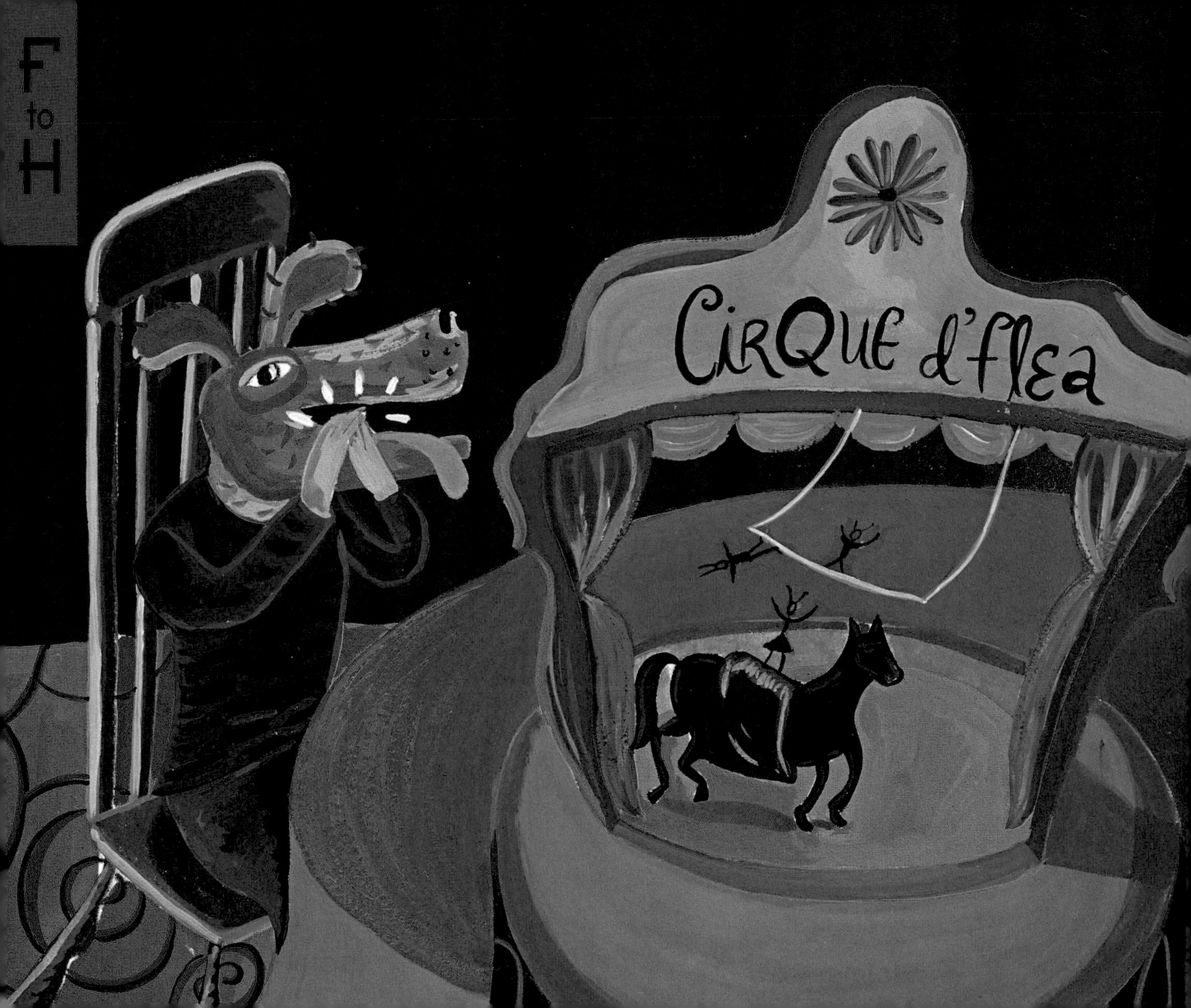
CIRQUE d'flea

FALSE PREGNANCY

Your dog will *look* pregnant. Her nipples will swell, and she will hide stuffed toys, acting very possessive of them. False pregnancy occurs within six weeks of the end of the heat cycle and may be exhibited by females in breeding kennels where other dogs are actually mothering. The condition may also occur in high-strung or pushy females who want to be pregnant, even if they did not "take."

— *Homeopathy:* To short-circuit the cycle and return the dog to her normal state, try **Pulsatilla** in the 30th potency, every 12 hours for 3 doses.

Pulsatilla animals, like the windflower itself, are the sensitive, changeable type—one minute shy and coy, the next demanding and pushy. They enjoy being the center of attention, especially when they do not feel well. They are not usually thirsty, and they like to sit by an open window, as the warmth makes them worse. Pulsatilla gals like to prop their heads up on something.

Along with the false heat signs, physically the Pulsatilla animal might have bouts of diarrhea, especially after eating fatty foods, and their stools never look the same. Pulsatilla cats and dogs sweat profusely from their paw pads when they are nervous at the vet's office.

Sepia, in the 12th to 30th potency, and given 2–3 times daily, is another choice for false pregnancy. Sepia animals are very emotional, often sad, and sometimes irritable. Unlike Pulsatilla animals, who like company and attention when ill, dogs and cats who need Sepia almost always prefer being by themselves when they don't feel well. They also prefer the heat, sitting next to the heater or in the sun. Their body shapes may appear very pear shaped, with a "hanging-type" belly.

FEAR

Some dogs or cats become terrified of strange objects, unfamiliar places, the dark, cars, or just about anything. Our reassurances to them seem to fall on deaf ears.

According to Chinese medicine, fear may stem from a hereditary weakness involving the kidney or heart. Foods such as **Barley** and **Oats** nourish these organs and the nervous system. Adding 1 teaspoon to $\frac{1}{2}$ cup of these thoroughly cooked grains to the diet may help calm your animal. **B vitamins** and **Trace minerals** also nourish the nerves.

— *Flower essences:* **Rock rose** helps calm terror. **Mimulus** assuages fear, and **Larch** cultivates courage. Add 3 drops of 1 or all to the water bowl.

— *Homeopathy:* **Aconite** in the 30th potency is especially good for animals who bite when they are frightened, especially when going to the veterinarian. Use 1–3 pellets (depending upon the animal's size) 30 minutes before a vet visit to calm the animal.

Gelsemium in the 30th potency is good for the animal who becomes weak, shaking with fear in the rear legs. Use 1 dose.

FIV AND FeLV

These cat viruses attack the immune system, debilitating the cat initially with fever and fatigue. After the initial bout, some cats will progress to weight loss, chronic diarrhea, or intestinal disturbances. Others will have respiratory distress, swollen lymph glands, anemia, or intermittent fevers. Still others will become "carriers" and show no further signs except when stressed out.

— *Homeopathy:* During acute attacks, with *fever and respiratory* distress, 1–3 doses of **Phosphorus** 30c may be helpful. Animals who need Phosphorus are usually very outgoing, friendly, and open. They are sensitive to sudden weather changes, enjoy eating, like drinking cold water (sometimes from the toilet), but may throw it up shortly after drinking it.

With *vomiting and diarrhea,* especially if the animal is chilly and restless, **Arsenicum album** in the 12th to 30th potency may be helpful. These animals may be thirsty, but they will only drink a few sips at one time. There may be blood in the vomit or stool.

With *diarrhea and abdominal bloating,* along with stomach gurgling, 1 dose of **Lycopodium** in the 12th to 30th potency may be called for. The Lycopodium female is the Marilyn Monroe type—very glamorous, but insecure underneath. The Lycopodium male may be "all bark and no bite." Physically, Lycopodium animals may have mucus-coated stools and feel worse between 4:00 and 8:00 P.M.

— *Herbs:* While the animal is seemingly healthy, strengthening tonic herbs are helpful. Use combinations available at your health food store containing **Astragalus, Siberian ginseng, Lycium berries, Tang kuei,** and **Ganoderma mushrooms.** The cat dosage should be ¼–⅓ the recommended human dose.

FLEA BITE DERMATITIS

Sensitive animals usually have weakened immune systems. These same animals may have recurrent ear infections, sensitive digestive tracts, or inhalant allergies. The flea is just the latest insult to the system that is already flagging.

— *Topicals:* Skin irritations that occur when fleas jump on and off an animal can create a miserable environment for both you and your dog or cat.

To soothe skin redness or rashes, use one of the following teas: **Black, Green, Chrysanthemum, Calendula,** or **Chamomile,** steeped at 1 teaspoon to 1 cup water and cooled, strained, and placed in a sprayer bottle to be applied lavishly. Or, you can apply the tea with a cloth. **Aloe vera gel** also acts as a cooler and soother, as do crushed fresh leaves from **Cleavers**, if you are so lucky to have these plants growing in your garden.

Foot soaks made from 1 tablespoon **White vinegar** or **Sodium bicarbonate** dissolved in 3 cups water can change the pH of the area, dissuading your animal friend from licking its paws.

— *Nutritional:* **Vitamin E** at 50–400 IU daily, depending upon the size of the animal, along with essential fatty acids at 1/2 the human recommended dose, can strengthen the immune system and decrease inflammation.

Quercitin at 125–250 mg daily, along with **Bromelain** (from pineapple) at 50–100 mg can also decrease inflammatory reactions.

— *Homeopathy:* **Sulphur** at the 6th to 12th potency may be given when the animal is severely itchy or red, or when blood comes from scratching eruptions.

Animals who need Sulphur may be lethargic, have bouts of diarrhea, and have very red anal openings. The animal's skin is usually dry and somewhat odoriferous.

Sulphur animals are very thirsty, drinking large amounts of water at one time. Sulphur might also be considered if your animal licks its paws obsessively. If Sulphur is given too frequently, it may worsen the situation, so use it sparingly.

(Also see *Skin Conditions* and *Itching*.)

— *Herbs:* Liver-clearing herbs such as **Burdock** and **Yellow Dock** roots that cool the skin and promote circulation, along with lymphatic herbs such as **Red Root**, can be helpful. Mix 10 drops of each tincture into 1 ounce distilled water, and give ½–1½ teaspoons twice daily, depending upon the size of the animal. Energy or Qi regulators such as **Lavender** and **Bergamot** can be added to the food to enhance digestion and circulation to promote healthy skin. Last, blood tonics such as **Nettles** and **Tang kuei** can be added to the food if the animal's skin is dry, flaky, and easily reddened.

— *Acupressure:* Three points may be helpful in cooling skin inflammation and relaxing the animal. The first is located on the front leg, at the outside end of the elbow crease when you flex the limb. The second is located on the back of the hind leg, in the crevice behind the knee. The third is located on the back of the head in the dimples below the ears. Rub each of these points for up to 1 minute twice daily.

FLEAS

If fleas paid their vet bills, I would have them for clients because there are so many of them!. Natural methods for flea control will repel, not necessarily kill, the fleas. To ensure the best results, treat the environment and your animal at the same time.

For your animal: Healthy animals seem to attract fewer fleas than those not in optimum health. Feeding a fresh diet with hormone- and pesticide-free meats, whole grains, and vegetables works for many animals. Include B vitamins such as B_1 and B_6, as found in synthetic form, Brewers yeast or chlorophyll products, along with 1 clove of garlic daily, help repel fleas.

Topical sprays with **Pyrethrins, Citronella, Lavender, Tea tree, Sage**, and **Mugwort** help repel fleas. Use several drops of each essential oil diluted into a carrier oil such as **Olive** or **Sesame,** and apply behind the neck, at the tail base, and a few dabs on the abdomen.

Bathing the animal in shampoos containing **Sodium laureth sulfate** in the lather and keeping the animal sudsed for 10 minutes will denude them of fleas.

For your home and yard: Several products are on the market to literally dehydrate or "dry up" the flea, such as **Diatomaceous earth,** which can be sprinkled in the yard. Dried **Nematodes** can be purchased through veterinary supply houses or garden stores. These are sprinkled on the premises and watered to wake them up.

A product called Precor that is a hormone to keep fleas as juvenile teenagers and prevent them from reproducing is incorporated in many new household spray products. This hormone can also be found at garden supply stores.

FOXTAILS AND SPLINTERS

Foxtails are long, sharp, sticky, burrlike plant pieces found on the West Coast. They can enter the body and migrate. Because of the barb at the end, they move only in one direction—inward, causing a severe inflammatory response. Migrating foxtails can create chronic conditions. If you see a foxtail enter a body hole such as the nose, eye, ear canal, or anus, bring your animal immediately to the veterinarian.

Another foxtail favorite entrance is between the toes or web of the animals' paws. Your animal might limp, or you might see a raised "pimple or blister" area that your animal is licking. Foot soaks, homeopathy, and herbs may be used to open a draining tract, relieve the pain, and retrieve the foxtail.

— *Topicals:* Soak first with **Epsom salts** and warm water. Follow with a topical poultice of **Plantain**, **Chickweed**, or **French clay**.

— *Homeopathy:* Internally, **Silica** in the 6th potency twice daily for up to 2 weeks can be used to keep a draining tract open and help expel the foreign body. If there is already an abscess brewing and the animal will not let you touch it, use **Hepar sulph** in the 30th potency. Two to three doses will probably be needed to open the wound. If there is a blood blister forming with a purplish color, 1 dose of **Lachesis** 30c may speed the process.

GAS/FLATULENCE

Passing gas is more common in dogs than in cats. You can usually hear it, if not smell it. Cats will silently discharge.

Since most dogs do not chew, but rely instead on hydrochloric acid production from the stomach to break down food, one source of gas is an inappropriate amount of acid. Gas can also stem from unbalanced enzymes in the small intestine, or from sluggish movement through the large intestine.

Food allergy can add to gas production, creating inflammation and deterring the passage of food through the gut.

— *Diet:* A diet change to a different protein source is the best first step. Making a home-cooked diet with small cubes of fresh meat requiring chewing, plus cooked grains and raw vegetables, may eliminate allergies that come from processed commercial foods. Pro-biotics such as **Lactobacillus Sporogenes** can help populate the gut with the good guys.

— *Herbs:* **Alfalfa** contains eight enzymes to help food break down. Add 1/4– 3/4 teaspoon per meal. **Oregano, Dill, Basil,** and **Garlic** help normalize stomach secretions, as does 1 drop of **Gentian**. **Papaya leaf** and **Aniseed** teas promote healthy digestion and decrease gas.

— *Massage* along the midline of the stomach, the inside of the thighs, and the hind legs to help stimulate movement through the intestinal tract and relieve gas.

GUM PROBLEMS AND GINGIVITIS

Red or bleeding gums can be painful, as well as destructive to the teeth. Diets that include bones or raw vegetables help gums stay healthy. Some dogs may benefit from gnawing on raw carrots, celery, knuckle, or short rib bones. I find that cats do better with chicken neck bones that have been cooked in their own broth.

— _Herbs:_ Gum washes of **Myrrh, Plantain,** and **Red raspberry** made into a tea and sponged on the gums with a gauze pad daily help restore sore gums.

Vitamin C at 100–750 mg daily and **Vitamin E** at 50–400 IU daily help decrease inflammation.

— _Acupressure:_ Use a point on the front paws in the web between the dew claw and main paw. If the dew claw was removed, find the "nub" of the bone where it was removed, and press between it and the main paw.

HIGH-STRUNG

In olden times, this condition was attributed to females as being "nervy." Today, males and females may suffer from short fuses that make them mean, teary, anxious, or overly alert.

If your animals jump at loud noises, bark at everything, bolt for cover when someone enters the house, or attack from fear when someone touches them, I would consider them "high-strung." The condition may reflect family emotional stress factors, or diets that wear the fluids (and thus calming capacity) down in the

body. An example of a "hot, drying" diet would be a dry food with a lamb protein source. Both the drying process and the lamb can create heat and drying out in the body. Animals need a certain fluid level to maintain equanimity. Without it, they can have short fuses or become high-strung.

— *Diet:* Changing the diet to include the "cooler proteins," such as cod, whitefish, or pork, and minimizing lamb and corn, may provide a calming effect Feeding turkey with its tryptophan may also help the condition. Also, try adding $1/4$–$1/2$ teaspoon of pickled cucumbers or strained green beans to the diet, and sprinkle the food with chamomile flowers.

— *Flower essences:* **Impatiens, Mimulus,** and **Red clover** help with nervousness, fear, and tension, which play roles in the animal's high-strung nature. Use 1–3 drops of each in your animal's water bowl for up to 3 weeks.

HIP DYSPLASIA

Hip dysplasia is a hereditary condition that affects many large and pure-bred dogs. Hip dysplasia creates severe arthritis in the hip joint that forms due to a poor angle of attachment between the hind limb and the pelvis. In some cases, the conformation is so poor that the hip ball does not fit into the socket at all.

— *Acupressure:* Massage three points surrounding the hip: in front of it, behind it, and on top of the joint. An acupressure point behind the knee joint in the groove between the muscle groups help reduce pain and strengthen the leg. (Also see *Arthritis.*)

— *Homeopathy:* Especially helpful are **Rhus toxidendron** for the animal who is painful yet seems to "warm out of it" once they are up and moving or **Bryonia** if any movement creates more discomfort. For short-term muscle soreness, use **Arnica montana** in the 30th potency.

HIVES

This is an acute allergic reaction where the dog expresses heat from inside the body that has come to the surface. Hives can look like raised hard bumps that make the hair stand up. They can also be bright red bumps you see on the abdomen. As long as hives are not accompanied by breathing distress, home care can be tried.

See if you can find the insulting cause. A weed on a recent walk? A new food? Sudden stress from family issues?

— *Homeopathy:* **Urtica urens** (stinging nettles) in the 6th to 30th potency is especially useful for itching, burning eruptions. Use 1 dose every 20–30 minutes for a total of 3 doses, and repeat a dose 6 hours later.

Apis mel in the 10th to 30th potency is especially useful for the dog or cat who has broken into hives after being out on a run or when it is very hot outside. Use 1 dose every hour for a total of 3 doses.

Histaminium is a homeopathic histamine that is what the body itself produces during an allergic reaction. Use the 6th potency every half-hour, for a total of 3 doses.

HOT SPOTS

These are intense areas of heat and oozing that rise to the skin's surface in what appears to be an instant. Some require veterinary assistance, while others can be treated at home

Gently clip the hair away. These areas are extremely sensitive and *hot*. So, be patient and careful. Spray the area copiously with cooled green tea, followed by **Calendula** and **Hypericum** tea, using ½ teaspoon of each in 1 pint boiled water. Then strain and cool. Repeat the green tea. **Calendula ointment,** powdered **Echinacea, Aloe vera,** or **Egg white** can then be applied topically.

HYPOTHYROIDISM

This metabolic disease affects some dogs through heredity. Pure-bred lines such as golden retrievers and dachshunds seem quite prone to developing hypothyroid disorders. Other potential causes may be attacks on the immune system, resulting from the overuse of Western medications such as antibiotics, chemical flea products, repeated vaccinations, or other toxic buildup—all of which ask the immune system to work harder.

Hypothyroidism will cause sluggishness, a dull and breaking coat, and weight gain.

This disorder usually requires thyroid supplementation under the guidance of your veterinarian. Holistic measures that you may try first, or in addition, include using a natural diet with whole or flaked grains, such as oats, cooked kidney beans, organic meat, and green leafy vegetables such as kale nourish the thyroid.

— *Herbs:* **Astragalus** plus **Siberian ginseng** are excellent vitality tonics that enhance energy and metabolic rate. Use tinctures, diluting 25 drops in 1 ounce spring water, giving ½– 3 teaspoons of the diluted mix.

Nettles, using ¼–¾ teaspoon daily, will nourish the blood and circulation..

Oregon grape root helps stimulate the liver and the thyroid gland. It is a strong, bitter herb, and only small amounts need be given, especially in the springtime, the *season* that influences the liver in Chinese medicine. Use 15 drops diluted in 1 ounce of spring water, shake 18 times, and give 1–2 teaspoons of the dilution twice daily for 10 days. The treatment can be repeated every 6 weeks.

— *Homeopathy:* Constitutional prescribing is best with an experienced practitioner. As a dog parent, you might try homeopathic **Thyroid-thyroidinum** at the 6th potency, using 1–3 pellets once daily for up to 2 weeks to "kick-start" the system.

— *Nutritional:* **B$_{12}$**, **Niacin**, **L-tyrosine**, **Iodine**, and **Copper** all support thyroid metabolism. Use supplements at ¼–½ the human recommended dosage.

I
to
J

tch

IMMUNE SYSTEM

Supporting the immune system can be done through any of the natural modalities. Acupressure massage is especially helpful and simple to add to any regimen.

— *Massage* along the inside of the lower hind leg area between the ankle and the muscles, especially in the triangle that feels like two pieces of skin rubbing together. An acupressure point located on the outside of the hind leg in the muscle below the knee increases vitality, while massaging around the front leg wrist in a circular direction can increase heart strength.

INCONTINENCE

As animals age, or if they were spayed or neutered at an inappropriate age, they may begin to lose control of their bladder. You may find puddles in the bed, on the rug, or on the couch, or they may "dribble" while walking around. Sometimes you may only see them licking their "privates" in an attempt to drink the escaping urine or to hide the scent.

Often a lack of estrogen or testosterone is causing the problem. Synthetic estrogens may help, but they might weaken the immune system.

— *Nutritional:* Foods that strengthen the kidneys or bladder, as well as the muscles in general, such as oats, chicken, and lamb kidney, may be added to the diet. Adding ½ teaspoon of chopped fresh kale, chive, and parsley to the diet strengthens the kidneys.

INCONTINENCE, cont'd.

— *Herbs:* **Schizandra fruit** is known as the "five-flavor seed" in Chinese medicine and acts as an "astringent" to hold the urine where it belongs and help curtail leaking. It is available in many health food stores and Chinese pharmacies. Use 5 drops of the tincture dissolved in $\frac{1}{2}$-ounce water, giving $\frac{1}{2}$–2 teaspoons twice daily depending on your animal's size.

Mullein leaf, using $\frac{1}{2}$ teaspoon to 1 cup of boiled water, steeped for 20 minutes, helps to tone bladder muscles, especially if a low-grade infection is suspected. Give 2 tablespoons of the diluted mix after the evening meal and before the last walk of the evening.

ITCHING

Itching can be extremely irritating for your animal, and it can drive you both to lose hair and sleep. Itching and skin problems mirror what is happening on the inside of the body. It is a metabolic problem and best treated by your holistic practitioner. Cortisone can always be used to stop the itch. Unfortunately, it weakens your animal's liver, kidney, and immune system, making your animal vulnerable to metabolic problems and infection. Cortisone should be avoided or kept to an extremely low dose unless absolutely necessary to prevent total misery.

Symptomatic and holistic treatment can use nutritional supplements, diet, herbs, and homeopathy. Please remember that the itch is a symptom reflecting an internal imbalance, and rebalancing should be the primary focus.

— *Herbs:* **Burdock root** is especially helpful for the animal who overheats easily and feels very hot to the touch. The skin is very red. Use it with **Cinnamon twig**, boiling 1 teaspoon of root and ¼ teaspoon twig for 20 minutes in 1 pint of water, and adding 1 teaspoon dried **Calendula** flowers during the last 5 minutes. Use 1–3 tablespoons twice daily for 2 weeks.

— *Topicals:* Sprays made from **Black** and **Green teas, Calendula flowers,** or **Chrysanthemum** help stop the itch.

— *Homeopathy:* Finding the constitutional remedy is the surest bet to stop the itch. You will need the assistance of a professional. Symptomatically, try **Sulphur** at the 6th, 12th, or 30th potency once daily for up to 1 week. If the itching intensifies, stop the remedy and wait several days to see if the body will balance out.

(Also see *Skin Problems* and *Hot Spots*.)

JAUNDICE

This serious problem is best handled under the care of your veterinarian. Your cat or dog will get jaundiced, with a yellow skin, mouth, and eye coloring when the bile ducts connected with the liver are blocked. In addition to conventional treatment, herbs and homeopathy can help your animal feel more comfortable and possibly speed up the process of opening the ducts.

— *Herbs:* **Milk thistle** is an excellent herb to nourish the liver and to reduce swelling in the bile ducts. It contains flavonoids and sylimarin flavonol, which decongest and restore liver tissue to a more normal state.

JAUNDICE, cont'd.

Use the dried herb if possible, as the tincture contains alcohol that may be harsh for the liver. Give 25 mg for a cat or small 10-pound dog, and up to 100 mg for a 60-pound dog twice daily for up to 1 month.

Burdock and **Yellow dock** roots made as slow-boiled teas help to clear the ducts and reduce swelling. Use 1 teaspoon of each root, boiled in 1 pint of water for 20 minutes. Give 1–3 tablespoons of the tea 3 times daily for up to 2 weeks.

— _Homeopathy:_ **Chelidonium** in the mother tincture (3–4 drops diluted in ¼ cup water) or the 6th potency given once or twice daily helps the animal who doesn't want to move around, or that feels worse with a change of weather. There may be vomiting, pain behind the shoulder blades, or a tight abdomen that feels better when you rub it.

Natrum sulphuricum (Nat sulph) in the 6th potency given once or twice daily is helpful for the animal who feels worse in damp or rainy weather. Animals who need Nat sulph may live in a constant damp environment and be prone to having skin or moist cough problems. These animals have a lot of gas and rumbling in the abdomen.

JEALOUSY

Jealousy is a trait more common to humans than dogs or cats. However, after living with _us_, this emotion seems to have rubbed off on them. Jealousy usually stems from fear—not having enough love or attention, especially in multi-animal households or when you get a new lover or mate who appears to "displace" the animal.

Quality time spent with your animal friends is the best way to handle jealousy.

— *Flower essences:* Add a few drops each of the flower essence **Mimulus** for fear, and **Walnut** for acceptance of change, plus a drop of **Quaking grass**, a California flower essence that helps deal with harmony within the household.

Jealousy can also stem from anger, especially if the animal is the assertive type who expects to get its way. Also, look at yourself, as we often attract the animal into our lives who acts out our inner feelings. When you come from a place of compassion and understanding, you may be able to change the energy of the animal-human bond.

Also, adding several drops of **Holly** for jealousy stemming from anger, **Chicory** for possessiveness, and **Vine** for inflexibility will help this situation.

Mix the essences in a water bowl, and stir to activate them.

MASSAGE
YOUR
DOG + CAT

KENNEL COUGH

This is an upper respiratory infection that your dog comes down with after being in social situations—at the park, dog shows, or at the kennel. Your dog will be slightly tired, possibly have a sore throat that you will notice because there might be problems swallowing food, or a lot of drooling from the corners of the mouth. The cough sounds honking or gaggy—like something is caught in the throat. It is usually a self-limiting virus, lasting about 2 weeks. If your dog's immune system is healthy, the virus will not go down to the lungs.

— *Nutritional:* Support the immune system using **Vitamin C** at 250–750 mg twice daily depending upon the size of the dog, and **Quercitin**—a bioflavonoid especially effective for the respiratory system. Use 75–125 mg twice daily. It works synergistically with the Vitamin C.

Evening primrose oil at 100–250 mg daily can be used to soothe inflamed cilia in the windpipe.

Aged **Garlic** at 100–200 mg once to twice daily will act as a natural antibacterial.

— *Herbs:* **Wild cherry bark** with **Mullein, Licorice,** and **Elecampane** help soothe the throat, relieve the cough, and protect the lungs. Make a tea, boiling 1 pint of water with 1 teaspoon Wild cherry bark, and ½ teaspoon Dried licorice root. Boil the bark and root for 20 minutes, then add the Mullein leaf for 10 minutes more. Cool and add 3 drops Elecampane tincture. Give 1 teaspoon 3–4 times daily for up to 1 week.

— _Homeopathy:_ **Spongia** in the 6th to 30th potency helps the animal with the hacking and loud, gagging type cough that gets worse as a result of barking or getting excited.

Kennel cough nosode in the 30th potency, available through holistic veterinarians and various health food stores, can be used once or twice to shorten the duration of the illness, or to prevent it from occurring if you need to put your dog in a kennel.

KIDNEY WEAKNESS

Signs of kidney weakness can arise as a result of age, or through heredity. Your animals may always be thirsty and _tanking up_, or they may be urinating too much or too little. They may have a difficult time with weather changes—panting when it's hot, or sticking close by the heater when it's cold. You may also see them vomiting food or mucusy water shortly after eating or drinking, or having trouble passing dry, crumbly stool.

As the kidney in Chinese medicine also includes bone development, all arthritis and bone problems can reflect an underlying kidney weakness. Acupuncture-pressure, herbs, and homeopathy can help the kidney patient.

— _Acupressure:_ Massage along either side of the backbone in the mid-body to help nourish the kidneys and stomach. Use light pressure in the mid-spine in the dimples between the last two ribs (where they meet the backbone), and continue

this pressure down to the middle of the low back. Acupressure on the insides of the hind ankles in the triangle formed between the Achilles tendon and the bone helps support the kidneys.

— *Herbs:* **Borage** is helpful for the thirsty and dry animal who has sparse urine, constipation, and, perhaps, a dry cough. This is the animal who will heat up very easily. Use the fluid extract from the leaf, diluting 15 drops in 1 ounce water and giving 1–3 teaspoons of the diluted mix once daily.

Nettles is helpful for the dry animal whose coat is very dull and flaky and whose energy is minimal. There may also be some swelling in the abdomen, so the animal looks slightly *pear-shaped*. Use the freeze-dried form from the fresh plant, giving 1/8–2/3 teaspoon once daily, depending on your animal's size.

Six-flavor tea pills, the famous Chinese patent medicine formula for kidney support, includes the herb **Rehmannia** (Chinese foxglove), which nourishes the kidneys. Available at many health food stores and through Chinese pharmacies, you can give 1–4 small round pellet pills once daily. If diarrhea develops, decrease the dosage.

— *Diet:* Barley is especially helpful to the kidneys, being salty and promoting fluid formation. Millet, string beans, peas, and soybeans, as well as potatoes or sweet potatoes, also build up fluids. Fluid-building foods are good for the *dry and hot* animal.

— *Homeopathy:* Constitutional prescribing by a professional homeopathic practitioner ensures the best result in chronic kidney conditions. The following remedies may be helpful in making your animal feel more comfortable. When using remedies

for kidney patients, less is always better. So use the remedy once daily for 3 days, and wait to see how the animal responds. You can repeat it weekly if it seems helpful for energy and water balance.

Natrum muriaticum (Nat mur) in the 6x potency is especially good for the animal who looks pear-shaped and malnourished. The muscles just seem to droop, and the belly seems to hang down. Your dog or cat might alternate between dry, crumbly stool and painless diarrhea. The animal is very thirsty and likes salty foods, especially commercial dry foods or pretzels. The dog or cat may seem sad to you and not want company or to interact with the family. Animals who need Nat mur enjoy the open air and sit near the window or the door in order to catch the breeze.

Calcarea carbonica in the 6th potency helps animals who are cold and like to sit by the heater. They can't stand the rain, and they pant while going up stairs or hills. They may have been the "runts" of the litter. There may be vomiting and loose stool, pains in the back, or hip dysplasia and arthritis. These animals seem anxious, and if they were humans, they might complain of heart palpitations.

Arsenicum album in the 12th potency is especially suited for the "fraidy cat" who jumps, runs, and hides all the time. The animal is restless and will move around frequently. These animals love being warm and may even singe their fur from sitting too close to the fire or over the pilot light on top of the stove when you're not cooking. Although they are thirsty, they like drinking small sips at a time.

KNEE PROBLEMS

The knee is the weight-bearing joint of the back leg. It is also full of ligament attachments. Proper bone metabolism and nutrition for the ligaments is essential to healthy knees.

Arthritis of the knee can be hereditary, stemming from poor alignment of the bones or from back problems that create muscle tension and an irregular angle around the knee joint. Twisting-type exercises such as Frisbee-catching on the run, quick turns, or jumping without proper warm-ups can also injure the knee. Be smart, and work up to exercising your animal. Please remember that sitting on the couch all week may not be good preparation for an all-out run, jump, and turn routine.

— *Nutritional:* All the antioxidants help in knee problems. (See *Arthritis.*) Additionally, **Alfalfa** and **Seaweeds** help nourish the ligaments and tendons.

— *Homeopathy:* Use remedies as infrequently as possible, giving the body time to respond. Once or twice weekly might be sufficient. Other animals may only need a dose once every 2 to 4 weeks. Let your animal tell you when re-dosing is needed. They will exhibit lameness or discomfort that is not relieved by massage. Dosage can be in the 6th to 30th potency.

Calcarea carbonica is good for animals whose knees feel worse in cold, wet weather and from going up stairs or hills.

KNEE PROBLEMS, cont'd.

Rhus toxidendron helps animals that feel bad upon rising and then feel better once they walk around. The lameness will return if they overexert themselves.

Ruta graveolens helps in situations where any kind of motion creates pain.

— *Acupressure:* Massage a point directly behind the knee joint in the crevice that forms when you bend the leg. Also, massage around the knee cap and down the leg, stopping on the outside of the ankle joint, in the dimple between the bone and the Achilles tendon.

LABOR, PREGNANCY, AND LACTATION

To keep the uterus happy and healthy, and to ensure that the afterbirth will be expelled promptly, give 1/2 teaspoon to 1 tablespoon **Red raspberry** leaves daily during the second half of pregnancy.

Lovage root acts as a uterine stimulant and can relieve pain before and during labor. Mix 15 drops tincture with 1 ounce water, and give 1–3 teaspoons every hour to relieve pain.

If there has been considerable trauma during the birthing process, **Shepherd's purse** can be used for hemorrhaging and to strengthen vaginal and uterine tissue. Topical application with gauze pads soaked in a strong tea of the herb, or letting your animal sit in its herbal bath can help with vaginal tears, while the powdered herb taken by mouth, 1/4–3/4 teaspoons, 3 times daily for several days can be beneficial for uterine health.

To increase milk production, add $\frac{1}{4}$–$\frac{1}{2}$ teaspoon **Nettles, Alfalfa, Cumin,** or **Aniseed** to the diet 1–2 times daily. Aniseed also helps to break up coagulated milk in the mammary glands.

Motherwort helps bring joy to nursing mothers and calms them in preparation for nurturing their young. It helps first-time mothers acclimate to motherhood. Use it as the dried, powdered herb, mixing $\frac{1}{2}$–1 teaspoon into $\frac{1}{4}$ cup grape juice and feeding 2–3 times daily to nursing mothers the first few days after the young are born to help the nursing process.

(Also see *Mammary Glands.*)

LIVER HEALTH

The liver is the largest body organ that works to clear toxins. It is also one of the main organs facilitating proper digestion, working with the stomach, pancreas, and gall bladder. Improper eating habits tax the liver and create pain during digestion.

In Chinese medicine, it is said that the liver and the eyes are associated, and that healthy eyes reflect a healthy liver. It is also said that the liver is most sensitive to insults during the springtime and in windy environments.

— *Diet:* Young, green leafy vegetables, especially dandelion greens, keep the liver circulation clear. A small amount of grated radish, along with celery and carrots, will help bile secretion. Bitter foods such as romaine lettuce and asparagus

LIVER HEALTH, cont'd.

relieve swelling in the liver. As there are numerous types of liver syndromes, each requiring a different treatment, you might refer to my book *Four Paws, Five Directions* for more in-depth treatment.

— *Herbs:* A mixture of **Milk thistle + Chamomile + Lavender** helps restore liver circulation and support liver cells. Mix $1/2$ teaspoon dried Milk thistle, with $1/4$ teaspoon Chamomile, plus $1/16$ teaspoon Lavender, and fill #3–#0 capsules, giving 1 daily, depending on your animal's size, for 2 weeks in springtime.

LUNG HEALTH

The lungs give us oxygen to carry out bodily functions. As we age, the lungs lose their elastic nature, making it harder to expand and collect the oxygen.

— *Nutritional:* **Vitamins A** and **E** nourish lung cell elasticity, while **Vitamin C** acts as a natural broncho-dilator, maximizing oxygen uptake. Use $1/2$– 2 teaspoons **Cod liver oil,** depending on the animal's size, to meet the Vitamin A requirement. Vitamin C should be used in as high a dose as possible without causing diarrhea, usually up to 1,000 mg.

Evening primrose oil, at 125–300 mg daily, furnishing natural Vitamin E, decreases inflammation and scar tissue buildup in older lung cells.

ACUPRESSURE

MASTITIS AND MAMMARY GLANDS

Mastitis can occur during nursing (from sharp teeth) or following heat cycles, whenever hormone levels are out of balance. It can also occur after trauma to the mammary glands.

The first stages can include pain and swelling of the gland and nipple. The animal will not want the young to suckle due to pain, and you may see cracked, crusted nipples with a clear fluid or puslike discharge. The milk may smell sour.

— *Topical applications:* Warm to room temperature compresses with **Dandelion** tea made from the leaves help to draw swelling out and cool the area. For very inflamed hot mammary glands, with an oozing discharge, a poultice from crushed moist **Plantain** or **Yarrow** leaves can reduce the inflammation and soothe the nipple.

— *Herbs:* The roots of **Dandelion** or **Burdock** help detoxify the infection and inflammation. Give 1–3 #0 capsules 3 times daily for 10 days, depending upon the size of the animal.

Red clover is helpful where there is a single cyst or nodule in one of the glands. Use the tincture, mixing 20 drops in 1 ounce distilled water, giving ½–2 teaspoons twice daily for 10 days. Red clover contains coumarins, so if there is a history of a bleeding disorder, use this herb only under the guidance of your veterinarian.

— *Homeopathy:* Remedies can be used every 2–3 hours during intense swelling and pain, and 3 times daily for 3–7 days after. If no relief is found after 3 doses, try another remedy or consult your veterinarian.

Lac caninum in the 6th to 30th potency helps in cases where the animal feels pain as the result of any touch or movement.

Hepar sulphuris in the 6th or 30th potency is helpful if there is pain upon touch and a cheesy, foul-smelling discharge from the nipple. Usually the animal is sensitive to cold and will want to sit near a heater.

Phytolacca in the 15th to 30th potency can be used if there is a rock-hard swelling in the mammary gland. The animal will be restless, with alternating fever and chills.

MOIST PAWS

Although animals naturally sweat through their paw pads, especially with anxiety, excessive sweat may create a growth environment for fungus. Moist paws, believe it or not, may also reflect poor digestion.

— _Diet:_ Adding drying foods such as rye flakes or amaranth or "water-balancing" fish such as mackerel, whitefish, or carp to the diet can strengthen the digestion and fluid balance in the body.

— _Topicals:_ Foot soaks with apple cider vinegar at 1 teaspoon to 1 cup of water, lemon water made from 1 lemon sliced into 1 pint of water, or baking soda solutions made from 1 tablespoon to 1 pint of water help to dry the paws and change the pH, discouraging fungal growth.

Tea tree oil and **Thuja occidentalis tincture soaks** both fight fungus. These are available through health food stores. Use 20 drops tincture to 1 cup of water, and soak the paws.

MOTION SICKNESS

If your animal gets queasy in the car, or outright vomits as you are tooling down the highway, using **Ginger** may be helpful. Make a tea from 1 slice of raw ginger root steeped for 10 minutes in 1 cup boiling water. Give 1–3 tablespoons a half-hour before the car ride.

— *Homeopathy:* **Cocculus** in the 6th to 12th potency, given once 20 minutes before travel may eliminate the feeling of dizziness and nausea that your animal may experience on a car ride. Lip smacking or frequent swallowing may be the only signs you see of the discomfort. Cocculus can be repeated at half-hour intervals for 3 doses.

Nux vomica in the 6th potency helps with nausea and dizziness. The animal is usually the irritable type, or may become that way after car rides.

MOURNING, GRIEVING, AND SADNESS

Grieving when your animal friend passes away is as natural as grieving for any other family member. Feel free to cry, memorialize, laugh, and share stories about your trusted companion with friends.

— *Flower essences and homeopathy:* If your animal friend has lost a family member, whether two-legged, four-legged, or winged, mourning or grieving is definitely part of its healing process.

To allow healing to occur on the emotional level so it will not manifest physically, use **Star of Bethlehem** flower essence. The clumps of small white Star of Bethlehem flowers only open in the sunshine, and when used homeopathically as the flower essence, it can restore the sunshine inside. Flower essences allow the animal to feel the emotion *and* work through it in order to maintain health. Mix 10 drops into 1 ounce of distilled water in a dropper bottle. Shake the bottle against the palm of your hand to *activate,* and give the animal 1–3 droppers daily for up to 2 weeks. Alternatively, add 3 drops to a small water bowl, stir, and change daily.

Borage flower essence can also be used to uplift the spirits.

Ignatia in the 30th potency, given once, will help the animal express shock, grief, or disappointment. This remedy is especially helpful if the animal appears to be sighing, swallowing, or yawning frequently.

MOUTHS, LIPS, AND TONGUES

Cracked lips in the corners of the mouth create irritation and discomfort for your animal. There may be bleeding and scabs, and if the dog or cat has a poochy type of face, bacteria can get caught in the folds of the face, causing a foul-smelling discharge.

Bathing the area with **Calendula flower tea**, followed by Calendula ointment applied to the area, will clean and re-grow normal tissue.

Poultices of powdered **Yellow dock root** help to decrease redness and swelling, while the young leaves are high in Vitamins A and C and can be added to the food to heal tissue.

Warts on the tongue can be from a virus and are usually unsightly, though not painful. Homeopathic **Thuja** in the 6th to 30th potency can be used to help the body work through the symptoms and rebalance itself. Use 3–4 doses of the 6th potency, or 2 doses of the 30th, spaced 24 hours apart. Wait up to 10 days for a response.

Ulcerations on the tongue may be an indication of a more serious problem such as stomach ulcers, kidney disease, or an immune-mediated problem. Please check with your veterinarian. If the cause is not one of the above, try changing the diet to include millet, vegetables, or light fish in order to change the pH in the stomach. Chlorophyll can be added to the diet, as well as acidophilus combinations to help improve the healthy gut flora.

Minor lacerations or cuts on the tongue can be treated with a topical dusting of powder of **Alum root** or **Psuedo ginseng** known as **Yunnan pai yao**, available at many health food stores or in Chinese pharmacies. Mouth rinses of **Horsetail** and **Yarrow** teas will also help staunch bleeding.

MUSCLE SPASMS, TIGHTNESS, AND TWITCHING

Muscle spasms can occur from lactic acid buildup after intense exercise, or from chronic bone problems that create constant irritation to the muscles.

— *Nutritional:* **Vitamin E** at 50 IU for cats and small dogs daily, to 400 IU for large dogs twice daily, helps to decrease muscle spasms.

Trace minerals including copper and molybdimum, and macro minerals of magnesium, calcium, and potassium help to calm twitching muscles.

— *Topical applications* of **Oil of lavender** or **Peppermint** disperses muscle soreness and tightness. Mix 5 drops Lavender or Peppermint to 20 drops **Olive oil,** and rub into spasming or tight areas.

— *Herbs:* **Teasle root** relieves tightness in muscles, especially in the large muscle groups such as the upper arm, thigh, or lower back. Mix 20 drops of tincture into 1 ounce of distilled water, using ½–1 teaspoon 3 times daily for 1 week.

NAIL AND TAIL SMASH

Have you ever been in such a hurry that you closed the car or bedroom door on your animal's tail or paw? Or, has Lucky ever come up lame after running free off-trail, holding up his paw with a claw hanging partly off? This situation occurs more frequently than you might think. It causes much discomfort and grief. Most of the time you will be able to handle the situation at home.

— *Homeopathy:* **Hypericum** in the 30c potency is the homeopathic form of St. John's wort and is *the* best remedy for nerve injuries to nails and tails, decreasing inflammation and increasing healing.

If the nail is hanging off at its base, exposing raw tissue underneath, clip the excess nail piece and bandage with a wrap of **Calendula** ointment mixed with several drops of **Hypericum** tincture. The wrap can be changed daily, soaking the injured area in a Calendula tea bath. Healing usually occurs within 10 days.

NAIL BED INFECTION

You will notice your animal limping gingerly or licking the toe and nail area intensely. You might also notice the odor—rotten or musty. The animal will be very protective of the area, making your inspection rather difficult.

If the condition is very severe, antibiotics and professional help may be necessary. However, I have found that most of these infections respond to 1 of 2 homeopathic remedies. If improvement is not seen after 3 days, or if the animal is running a high fever, please call your veterinarian.

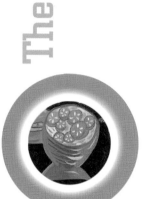

NAIL BED INFECTION, cont'd.

— *Homeopathy:* **Hepar sulphuris** in the 6th to 30th potency using 1 dose twice daily for 3–5 days helps the animal with a sour and offensive odor coming from the toe. The animal wants warmth and likes to burrow under the covers.

Hekla lava (volcanic ash) in the 6x potency used twice daily for 3–5 days is especially good if the toenail itself looks slightly deformed and the toe is swollen and painful.

NAIL CRACKING

This condition can be associated with poor blood circulation or blood stores. Adding 1/4–1 teaspoon of **Kelp powder** or other **Seaweeds,** 1/2–1 teaspoon **Biotin,** plus **Garlic** (which includes natural sulphur compounds to strengthen nails) may be helpful.

NECK PROBLEMS

Many animals who suffer from neck problems will be reluctant to bend down to drink water or eat food from the bowl on the floor. So, part of any treatment will include raising the feeding bowls up on steps or low tables.

Another sign you may see of a neck problem is the animal's reluctance to turn in one direction. Or, you may witness limping first on one front leg and then the other, so you are unsure which leg is affected. These animals are also hesitant to go downstairs because of weight bearing on one of the front limbs.

Neck problems tend to get worse during the winter when it is cold and damp. Having your dog wear a neck muffler/warmer protects this susceptible area, especially in short-haired breeds.

Acupuncture, acupressure, chiropractic, and massage of the muscles are all generally helpful, as they relieve tension and restore energy and circulation to the area.

— *Acupressure:* Hold or lightly press each point for 30–60 seconds, several times daily, especially before walks. Massage the points at the base of the back of the head, in the 2 dimples below and behind the base of the ears to help relieve neck pain.

Massage at the base of the front of the neck, just in front of the shoulder blades in the muscle dimples.

Hold the point on the outside of the front leg, at the end of the elbow crease, just in front of the bone, for 30 seconds.

— *Homeopathy:* For acute neck problems, **Belladonna** and **Arnica** help alleviate inflammation and associated pain. Use the 30th or higher potencies every 20 minutes for the first hour, then at 2-hour intervals for the first day. After that, 2–3 doses daily for up to 1 week are beneficial. Curtailing your animal's movements is also in order.

For chronic problems, remedies may be given once weekly. If no response is seen, try another remedy or check with your veterinarian.

Calcarea carbonica in the 6th to 12th potency helps those animals with stiffness

in the neck. They are reluctant to flex or turn to a specific side. Problems are usually worse with wet and cold weather. Animals who need Calcarea may prefer to be couch potatoes at home.

Causticum in the 6th to12th potency is another remedy that helps the animal who tends to exhibit stiffness in the neck. The animal may also lose feeling in one of the front legs and stumble over it frequently.

Rhus toxidendron in the 6th to 30th potency helps those animals who are restless and change position even though the neck is stiff and hurts. These animals are worse after resting and seem to improve after their first few steps, warming out of it. If exercise becomes too strenuous, they begin to hurt again.

Natrum muriaticum in the 6th to 30th potency helps the animal with weak neck muscles, where the animal's head appears heavy and the animal requires support.

NOISE SENSITIVITY

These animals will run and hide from loud noises such as the doorbell, telephone, or vacuum cleaner. Others are just terrified (understandably) of violent noises from firecrackers or car alarms, while some animals are sensitive only to high-pitched sounds.

Herbs that nourish the fluids of the body and calm the mind and heart give these animals relief.

— *Herbs:* A combination of **Oats, Nettles,** and **Motherwort** will help to nourish the blood and fluids of the body, calm the mind, and support the heart. Use 15 drops each of Oats and Nettles tinctures, and 9 drops of Motherwort, all diluted in 1 ounce of distilled water. Shake against the palm of the hand and give 1–3 droppers twice daily.

— *Flower essences:* Mix 3–5 drops each of: **Mimulus, Rock rose, Star of Bethlehem, Lavender,** and **Larch** into 1 ounce of distilled water, giving droppers freely during firecracker time. Mimulus, Rock rose, and Star all address fear, terror, and shock; while Larch fortifies courage, and Lavender harmonizes the rest of the flowers working together.

NOSE—see *Sinus Woes*

OBSESSIONS

Let's face it, some animals are just obsessive. It might have to do with a cooped-up lifestyle, or coping with intense 21st-century noise: construction, traffic, car alarms, or loud music. Some obsessions are hereditary, so they may be difficult to change. If being cooped up is the problem, make time in your schedule to get out more often with your animal.

Obsessions such as possessiveness of balls, bones, food, or toys may relate to an imbalance in the liver or central nervous system. They can also relate to a diet

OBSESSIONS, cont'd.

where the food is irritating to the stomach, with excessive hydrochloric acid production.

— *Diet:* Adding foods to calm the liver and stomach, such as well-cooked millet, brown rice, boiled potato, peas, cod, sole or whitefish will change the pH and regulate the flow of food passing through the stomach into the small intestine.

— *Flower essences:* Adding 3–5 drops of any or all of the following may balance the behavioral process.

Vervain is for the animal that is possessive, passionate, overenthusiastic, or downright overbearing.

Vine is for the domineering animal that wants things its way and wants others to follow.

Chicory is for the animal that needs to be the center of attention and wants all of *yours*.

— *Homeopathy:* The salts of phosphorus seem helpful in nervous-type conditions. Try **Natrum phosphoricum** or **Kali phosphoricum** in the 3rd to 6th potency, using either, or alternating between them once to twice daily for up to 3 weeks.

PACING AND PANTING

These behaviors can stem from pain or lung problems. They can also reflect a diminishing amount of fluid stores within the body, making the animal just "feel" hot. While it is not unusual for dogs to pant, when cats do it, it is an *emergency*. Take

your cat to the veterinarian immediately.

— _Diet:_ Decreasing or supplementing dry foods with fresh, moistening choices such as chopped green vegetables like cabbage, celery, lettuce, string beans; or peas, and potatoes, sweet potatoes, mushrooms, or barley can increase the body's fluid stores. Decreasing or eliminating chicken, lamb, or venison can also cool your animal down. Substitute pork, lean beef, sardines, whitefish, or bean curd to decrease agitation.

— _Herbs:_ Use ¼–⅔ teaspoon of any or all of these herbs depending on the size of your animal friend.

Alfalfa contains natural enzymes that ease cellular transactions and may relieve pain. Alfalfa contains calcium necessary for oxygen metabolism, muscle contractions, blood building, and circulation. Alfalfa also decreases cholesterol.

Oats contain minerals and saponins and are nourishing to the energy and fluids and calming to the heart, regulating anxiety and helping rest.

Chamomile calms the digestion and spirit.

PANCREATITIS

Acute pancreatitis requires emergency veterinary care, as the vomiting and inflammation may be life threatening.

For those animals with a chronic problem, acupressure, diet, and homeopathy may be added to any regimen your veterinarian recommends.

PANCREATITIS, cont'd.

— *Acupressure:* Apply gentle pressure for 30 seconds twice daily in the mid-back region, approximately a thumbnail's distance from either side of the backbone, in the muscle depression between the last two ribs and just behind the rib cage. Gentle massage on the belly mid-line halfway between the breastbone and the belly button (which on animals appears as a mild circular discoloration usually between the second and third sets of nipples) facilitates normal digestion.

— *Diet:* Buckwheat, which is high in rutin, helps decrease intestinal inflammation and strengthens blood circulation. Avoid foods high in fat, as these require pancreatic and liver enzyme interaction to break them down.

Nutritional supplements that contain raw **Pancreas enzyme** are helpful, as long as there are no duodenal ulcers, using $1/4$–$1/2$ the recommended human dose.

— *Homeopathy:* **Natrum sulphuricum** (Nat sulph) in the 6th potency taken daily for 1 week and then approximately once weekly will help the animal who feels worse in damp weather, in the evening, and with pressure or touch to the abdomen. Animals who need Nat sulph usually have a picky appetite and seem sad. They may also be light-sensitive and have streaming tears when exposed to direct sunlight. Their bellies rumble, and there may be flatulence.

Iris versicolor in the 6th to 30th potency is for the patient who is nauseated, drools ropy thick saliva, and may be vomiting sour-smelling fluid or bile. The animal may also have runny stool that it runs away from with seemingly a burning discomfort. Use 1 dose every 3 hours, up to 3 times during a more acute phase, and repeat only when the animal begins profuse salivation and seems nauseated.

PAW AND PAD PROBLEMS

Easily cracked and dry pads can reflect a deficiency of blood circulation or vitamin absorption. The tips of the extremities require strong blood-pumping action to reach the surface. Nourishing the tips of the limbs also requires good digestion and absorption of proteins and vitamins.

Licking of the pads and between the toes can result from an itchy contact allergy, or referred pain from back, limb, or stomach. Often, when animals cannot reach the painful spot, they'll resort to licking to soothe their frustration. Licking can also mean a circulatory malfunction, making the paws tingle like pins and needles.

— *Massage* gently between the webs of the paws and on the pads themselves to stimulate circulation, which is part of what your animal friend is trying to do anyway by constant licking.

— *Topicals:* **Vitamin E** or **Almond oil** lubricate the top layer of cracked pads, while high-protein **Egg white** strengthens them.

— *Nutritional:* **Vitamin B** complex, with extra **Biotin,** reinforces weak pads and fills in the cracks.

— *Homeopathy:* **Calcarea flourica** in the 6th to 30th potency may be given once weekly or every 2 weeks, for up to 3 doses to remedy the condition. The animal responsive to Calcarea flourica may also have chronic dental problems with poor enamel, thickened or misshaped nails, or varicose veins. The animal may also have an itch below its tail and want to scoot over the floor, leaving a blood-tinged trail.

PERFORMANCE ENHANCERS

Increasing stamina and enhancing musculoskeletal health require a boost of energy and excellent digestive absorption. Holistic modalities can keep your animal companion sleek and energetic.

— *Acupressure:* Massage the muscle on the outside of the hind leg just below the knee in a circular motion. This point, known as the "run three mile," was used by messengers in ancient China to increase their stamina running between camps.

Apply gentle pressure to the inside of the hind ankles at the top of the hollow between the ankle bone and the muscle to help digestive absorption.

Rub gently between the dew claw and paw of the front feet to fortify protection against upper respiratory infections and to stimulate the immune response.

— *Herbs* can be used regularly for long periods of time without harmful side effects. I recommend using these tonic herbs 5 out of 7 days a week; or 3 weeks on, 1 week off to keep your animal healthy.

Astragalus membranaceous is a Chinese herb now cultivated in the United States to increase energy and protect against infection. Use the liquid extracts, mixing 30 drops to 1 ounce distilled water, and administer $\frac{1}{2}$–1$\frac{1}{2}$ teaspoons of this mixture once daily depending upon your animal's size.

Siberian and **Korean ginseng** help the animal adapt to stress situations, including being left in the kennel. They also help to regulate fluid and energy. Use the powdered or pill forms, giving the equivalent of 100–250 mg daily.

— *Nutritional:* Both **Vitamin C** as sodium ascorbate or in the "ester"-form help

with performance and immune response. Use 50–1500 mg daily depending upon the size of the animal. If diarrhea develops, stop the vitamin, and begin again on 1/2 the dose you've tried.

Vitamin E with **Selenium** helps boost immunity and decrease joint inflammation. Use 50–400 IU daily Vitamin E, plus 10–50 mcg Selenium.

Co-enzyme Q10 helps with cell oxygenation and may increase stamina and breathing capacity. Use 10–30 mg daily.

Seaweeds supply minerals for cellular metabolism and can be given at $\frac{1}{8}$–$\frac{1}{2}$ teaspoon daily.

PROSTATE GLAND

Prostate inflammation or enlargement can plague your male dog, causing discomfort, stop-and-go urination, dribbling urine, or straining when having bowel movements. Since it is diagnosed via a rectal exam, your veterinarian will be the one to confirm the diagnosis and to advise whether surgical neutering is advisable. An enlarged prostate can block urination altogether and become life threatening. If your dog is showing any of these signs, it is wise to have your vet check them out.

Natural remedies can be used to shrink swelling and decrease inflammation, and as an adjunct to Western medical treatment.

— Nutritional: **Zinc pincolate** at 10–25 mg daily, depending upon the size of the dog, helps to regulate prostate health, along with a multiple **B vitamin** at $\frac{1}{2}$ the human dose.

PROSTATE GLAND, cont'd.

— _Herbs:_ **Saw palmetto + Cleavers + Echinacea**, mixing 15 drops of each into 1 ounce distilled water, will help decongest and soothe inflammation of the prostate gland. Give ½–3 teaspoons of this mixture 4 times daily during an acute situation, and then twice daily for 3 weeks.

almond oil

Vinegar

aniseed oil

EAR OIL

frieden

RINGWORM

This fungal disease of the skin is very itchy and has very round, scaly circles with a red rim. Ringworm can be transmitted from your animal to you, and looks similar. So, if you suspect it, and are susceptible, bring your animal to a veterinarian for professional assistance.

Since many animals are exposed to ringworm and don't get infected, it seems that only susceptible animals with compromised immune systems fall prey to it. Usually these include very young or old animals. Keeping the immune system in tip-top shape (check performance enhancers, immune system) is the best method for protection. If your animal *does* get it, these home remedies are helpful.

— *Herbs:* **Oregano leaf and flower** as a tea or tincture, diluted at 35–40 drops per ounce of distilled water, can relieve the itching and help rid the fungus. Use 1/2–1 1/2 teaspoons orally 3 times daily.

— *Topicals:* **Tea tree oil (Melaluca)** applied to the affected skin areas will kill the fungus and stop the itching.

— *Homeopathy:* **Thuja occidentalis** in the 12th to 30th potency given every 12 hours, 2–3 times, will usually stop the spread and slowly balance the immune system to overthrow the fungus.

Natrum muriaticum (Nat mur) in the 12th to 30th potency, given every 12 hours, 2–3 times, is good for the animal who is very thirsty and drinks large quantities at one time. The animal may have a history of a stuffy nose or creamy nose discharge. Physically, animals who need Nat mur often have a "pear-shaped" body, with hanging abdomen and thin, weak legs.

SINUS WOES AND SNEEZING

Sinus problems are some of the most challenging to deal with because of the huge surface area, many folds, and hiding places inside the nasal cavity. Infection can linger there; and inflammation, which continues even after the organism is gone, makes the membranes sore, swollen, congested, or bloody. Once a sinus problem takes hold, it usually takes a long time to resolve.

— *Acupressure:* One of the fastest ways to stop repeated sneezing and sinus inflammation comes from pressing a point deep in the web between the dew claw and the front paws. Press the point for approximately 30 seconds at a time, and repeat several times daily to build a more lasting response. This point also helps to relieve headaches from sinus congestion.

Pressing points around the eyes at 9:00, 12:00, 3:00, and 6:00 relieves pressure in the sinus and helps drainage through eye tearing.

Last, press a point at the base of the back of the head, in the dimples behind the base of each ear, to relieve pressure buildup.

— *Herbs* with volatile oils, such as **Oregano, Marjoram,** and **Thyme** are helpful to liquefy the phlegm and relieve congestion. These culinary herbs also have anti-microbial effects. Use them in a vaporizer, and steam the animal in a small room such as a bathroom for 10–15 minutes at a time.

Garlic, especially the aged preparations, are high in sulphur compounds and are naturally directed upward toward the head. Use $^1/_3$–$^3/_4$ the recommended human dosage on products, depending upon the size of the animal.

— *Homeopathy:* For chronic situations, use the 6th to 30th potency twice weekly, and assess its effect. If, after 3 weeks, there is no change, try another remedy.

Kali bichromicum is good for the animal with thick dry-type crusts. There may be serious sneezing spells in which the crust explodes on the wall or couch.

Natrum muriaticum (Nat mur) is good for the type of clear or "egg-white" mucus in the serious or analytical type of animal. Animals who need Nat mur do not seek the sun or heaters, and feel worse if you try to console them.

Pulsatilla helps the animal with yellowish or greenish nasal discharge, and when sinus problems are worse at night. These animals like sitting by an open window or going out at night, and when inside, prefer being high up on shelves (cats) or on the backs of couches. They may also have symptoms of asthma. Animals needing Pulsatilla like company and may be wishy-washy about making decisions, except that they absolutely do not like getting their paws wet.

— Nutritional: Antioxidants such as **Glucosamine** and **Chondroitin sulfates** help relieve bone inflammation in the sinus. Use $\frac{1}{4}$–$\frac{1}{2}$ the recommended human dose.

SKIN SORES AND SCABS

The skin reflects the entire body. This is why it is so challenging to treat, as any organ system can be involved. In fact, when your animal starts scratching and thumping, you often want to pull out your own hair to mirror the frustration.

The animal plagued with skin problems has an out-of-balance immune system, so nutritional and herbal supplements to strengthen the system should be part of any program you start.

Food allergies play their fair share in skin eruptions; experimenting with choices that include different animal or vegetable protein, using fresh raw foods, or rotating single grains or animal proteins can bring about rewarding results.

The liver is the largest detoxifying organ in the body and is invariably out of balance when skin problems arise. The heat generated by the liver internally can use up the body's fluid stores, making the animal red, itchy, thirsty and smelly. The greater the heat, the greater the odor.

— Diet: Add cooling-type foods such as dandelion greens, spinach, lettuce, celery, cucumber, and tofu to the diet. According to Chinese food therapy, adding peas to the diet helps to balance the liver with the other digestive organs, and helps eliminate skin eruptions. Apples and pears also cool and moisten.

Avoid a dry food-only diet. Even if you pour water over the top, the heating or fat-spraying process used in making dry foods creates huge amounts of heat within the body and makes the liver work hard to break up the fats.

— *Herbs:* Mix equal parts of the following herbs to assist liver functions and clear red, itchy skin, sores, and scabs.

Oregon grape root + Calendula + Yellow dock + Spearmint: Use ½–2 teaspoons 1–2 times daily depending upon the size of the animal for up to 2 weeks at a time.

Green tea extract tablets help to balance the immune system: Use ½–4 tablets once daily.

— *Topicals:* Solutions made from **Black** or **Chamomile tea**, cooled and placed in a spray bottle and applied lavishly on your animal's skin help relieve the inflammation. **Calendula** lotion or **Aloe vera gel** help soothe.

— *Homeopathy:* Constitutional prescribing by a professional yields the best responses. Combination remedies that improve the condition are also available at health food stores. You may also try one of the following:

Sulphur in the 6th to 30th potency help the animal with red, itchy skin, especially around the eyes, muzzle, or under the tail. There may be a sour odor to the skin, and the animal may itch the sores until they bleed. Animals responsive to Sulphur like to rub against the walls and under coffee tables to relieve the itch. They are usually very thirsty animals and may be prone to mucus in the stool, or easy diarrhea. They are the types who wake you at 5:00 A.M. to demand food and who crash at 11:00 A.M. for a nap. When you look at these animals, they often have the expression of being downright miserable about their condition.

After each dose of Sulphur, wait at least 3 days for a response. Try this up to 3 times. If you notice no effect, try a different remedy. If sulphur is helpful, you can repeat it at weekly intervals.

Psorinum in the 12th to 30th potency helps the dog or cat whose rancid, putrid skin odor can knock you out. There are usually multiple scabs or small slow-healing ulcers, loads of itching, and a clammy-type feeling on the skin. The ears can have

101

moist discharge and be very itchy. These animals loathe being cold and may singe their fur trying to be next to the fireplace.

This remedy should not be used often—just 1 or 2 doses of the 30th potency, and wait up to 1 month for a response.

STRAINS, SPRAINS, AND SPASMS

A strain happens when there is an *overstretching* of a muscle or muscle groups. This leads to muscle spasms, tightness, and possibly stiffness. A sprain involves a joint with ligaments that attach to the bones, such as when you sprain your ankle. Swelling, heat, and pain that is worse with movement usually occur.

Strains like warmth to relax the muscle and stop its repeated contractions. Sprains like ice, alternating with heat to relieve the swelling and relax the muscle attachments. They usually feel better being wrapped in a bandage.

— *Acupressure:* For muscle strain, using the *aspirin* acupressure point is helpful. This is located in the depression above the outside of the ankle on the hind leg. Hold this point for 30–60 seconds at a time.

For sprains involving the joints and ligaments, acupressure to strengthen these structures gives assistance. Use the aspirin point as mentioned above, and a point that is located on the outside of the hind leg, about midway down, just below the knee. You will feel a small dimple between the muscle groups. Hold this point for 30–60 seconds at a time.

— *Nutritional:* **Vitamin E** acts as a natural anti-inflammatory. Use 50–400 IU twice daily.

Glucosamines and **Chondroitin sulfate** relieve joint pain. There are special veterinary products, or you can use one of the human products at $\frac{1}{4}$– $\frac{3}{4}$ the recommended dose, depending upon the size of your animal.

Alfalfa at 100–300 mg 1–2 times daily relieves muscle spasms.

— *Topically:* Use small amounts of the following essential oils, diluted 10 drops to 1 tablespoon of a carrier oil, such as olive, working it gently into the fur, repeating several times daily.

Lavender or **Peppermint oil** if the animal feels better with something cool; **Clove oil** if the animal feels better with heat

— *Homeopathy:* In acute injuries, these remedies can be used every 20 minutes for the first two hours, then 2–3 times daily for up to 5 days.

Arnica in the 30th or higher potencies to control swelling and pain, and relieve muscle spasms.

Bellis perennis in the 30th or higher potency for pelvic or lower abdominal injuries and muscle spasms.

Ruta graveolens in the 6th to 30th potency for sprains of the ankle, wrist, or knee.

Hypericum in the 12th to 30th potency for nerve pain, especially around the low back, sacrum, or for toe or tail injuries.

TEETH

Even though your dog or cat may look like they are inhaling their food, they do need teeth to chew or tear it somewhat before it goes down to the stomach. The teeth are part of the skeletal system, and if your animal's bones and back have problems, they may also have teeth problems.

Many dogs will wear their front teeth down by chewing on toys, rocks, or themselves. If this is the case, please check "Obsessions," or notice if they have gas or grumbly tummies. The chewing may be part of their frustration at not feeling well or not getting enough exercise. Once the teeth are worn, there's very little to do about it.

Healthy teeth need healthy gums in order to prosper. Spongy or bleeding gums can also reflect dietary problems (also see *Gums* and *Mouth*).

Weak or loose teeth:

— *Diet:* Adding calcium and phosphorus in the form of bone meal helps to balance these 2 nutrients in the body. Use bovine products, egg or oyster shell, giving $1/8–3/4$ teaspoon depending upon your animal's size.

Green foods including chlorophyll provide the trace minerals needed for bone remodeling and health.

Foods high in sugar and fat interfere with calcium metabolism and, thus, bone renewal. So limit the treats, and check the ingredient content of the foods you are feeding.

Make certain your animal gets enough sunshine, as this helps with Vitamin D metabolism needed to start the calcium movement in the body. Fish oils from cod liver or herrings are high in Vitamin D.

— *Homeopathy:* **Calcarea phosphorica** in the 3rd to 6th potency on an every-other-day program for 1 month helps strengthen the teeth.

— *Herbs:* **Horsetail** is rich in silicon and helps to regenerate and nourish the bones and teeth. Use ⅛–⅔ teaspoon once every 10 days.

Teething: Often kittens or puppies have teething problems. This is especially true of the toy and small breeds. Homeopathy helps with pain and irritability. Often, only a couple of doses are necessary.

Chamomilla in the 30th potency helps animals who are irritable, crying, and demanding, but turn down anything you offer. The only thing that helps temporarily is picking them up and carrying them around.

Calcarea phosphorica in the 6th potency helps the animal who has problems with *double* canine teeth—that is, their new canines grow in, and the old ones remain right next to them, not falling out as is the normal process. These animals will often have tummy problems, with grumbling and burping.

Toothaches: With toothaches, you will notice that the animals look uncomfortable, and even if they are hungry, they will just stare at the food dish. They may hang

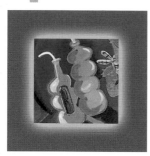

TEETH, cont'd.

their heads over or in the water bowl because the cool water decreases the pain. You might also smell very bad breath or see blood-tinged drooling.

Now there are veterinary dentists who are skilled in pulling teeth, dental surgery, or even filling decayed teeth. You might consult with your veterinarian on the best course of action. In conjunction with conventional treatment, homeopathy helps clear up the infection and relieve pain.

— *Homeopathy:* **Hepar sulphur** in the 30th potency is used for the animal who screams in pain when you try to open the mouth. The gums may be very red, and there is a puslike odor coming from the mouth. These animals shy away from food just out of the refrigerator or cold water touching the mouth.

Use 1–3 doses during the day, and evaluate by the following day. If there is no relief, try another remedy.

Silica in the 12th potency helps resolve tooth root abscesses in the timid type of animal. These problems may have developed slowly and may be accompanied by swollen glands in the throat. The animal is often chilly and very mild-mannered.

Ruta graveolens in the 6th to 30th potency helps after tooth-pulling to heal the empty space where the tooth attached to the jawbone. Use 1 dose hourly, for 3 hours following dental surgery, and repeat once the next day to ensure smooth healing.

UNDER THE TAIL

Many animals suffer from redness or rawness under the tail surrounding the rectal opening. The moistness that resembles sweating comes from diarrhea remnants or leaking anal glands. Redness and congestion can also occur with constipation, which protrudes from the mucous-membrane lining like human "hemorrhoids."

— _Diet_ plays a major factor, as the anus is the last part of the digestive tract. Adding fiber by including well-cooked peas or lentils to the diet removes excess moisture and congestion from the system.

— _Nutritional:_ **Psyllium husk** and **seed** help with bulk fiber and essential oils to regulate the moisture content of the colon and rectal area. Mix $1/8$–$3/4$ teaspoon dried herbs, depending upon the size of the animal, into the food..

Acidophilous combinations including F.O.S. and lactobacillus sporogenes help to populate the intestines with the good guys to regulate absorption of nutrients and promote a vibrant and healthy digestive tract lining.

— _Topical soaks_ made with **Calendula** using 1 teaspoon dried herb to 1 pint boiled water, steeped for 20 minutes and cooled, relieves congestion and inflammation. Calendula is known by many herbalists as "herbal sunshine," and according to herbalist Matthew Wood, it benefits body places "where the sun doesn't shine," like under the tail.

White oak bark tea helps with congestion and swelling, especially with the animal who has chronically loose stool, weak muscle tone, and a feeling of coldness (so they seek out the sun).

VAGINITIS

This is a problem usually with puppies or with older female dogs who also have urinary problems. In the puppies, it appears to be related to an out-of-balance immune system or a virus. Some holistic veterinarians attribute this condition to a vaccine reaction. In the older female dog, the musculature in the vagina may be weak, so that urine "pools" there, creating irritation and, potentially, infections.

You will notice the animal licking and grooming her "private parts" excessively. There will be redness, itching, dryness, or a thick ropy type discharge. She might also have trains of male dogs following her.

Although douching is helpful, it is sometimes difficult to get your dog to cooperate. If you *can* get her cooperation, local applications of **Green** or **Plantain tea** are helpful. Alternatively, oral herbal combinations or homeopathic remedies can tone the muscles and calm the vagina down. Since this problem may also stem from other causes, it is always a good idea to check with your veterinarian.

The following oral natural remedies can be used along with conventional therapy or by themselves.

— *Herbs:* **Yarrow + Oatstraw + Marshmallow root** help to relieve inflammation, soothe the tissue, and strengthen the vaginal tone. This combination will also help to dry discharge. Combine 9 drops each of the liquid extract/tincture into 1 ounce distilled water, using 1 teaspoon to 1 tablespoon 3–4 times daily for 1 to 2 weeks.

You can substitute **Gentian** for the yarrow.

— *Homeopathy:* Give 3 doses daily of either of the following remedies for up to 2 days to get a response. If no improvement is seen, seek professional assistance, as your animal will be miserable otherwise. If the remedy is helpful, however, you can continue this treatment for up to 1 week if necessary.

Kreosotum in the 6th to 30th potency is helpful for the animal with a red, inflamed, itchy, acrid discharge that burns off the hair around the vaginal opening. The skin looks very raw, and the animal does not want to be touched there. The odor is strong, with both you and male dogs noticing it.

Kali bichromicum in the 6th to 30th potency is good for the animal with a ropy, sticky, tough, and clear or light yellow vaginal discharge that may hang down the inside of the legs. The animal responsive to Kali bichromicum usually has a weak hind end and a history of bladder infections or stones.

VOMITING

Vomiting can be a serious problem, especially with animals who are "off-leash" and tend to eat foreign objects or garbage. Since foreign bodies may perforate the stomach or intestine, if you suspect that your animals have ingested hazardous materials, bring them to the vet. Dehydration can also occur with severe vomiting. So please monitor your animal.

In long-term situations, where your animal vomits weekly or occasionally or if there is an acute viral situation, homeopathy can be of tremendous assistance. Most

important, of course, is to make dietary changes, as vomiting is a sign of poor food absorption.

— _Homeopathy_: **Nux vomica** in the 6th to 30th potency is helpful for the irritable type "A" personality who gets stressed out easily. The vomiting may be violent with a huge amount of retching accompanying it. The animal tends to be a "garbage hound" with a loud bark or meow, and likes to be in charge. The animal does not necessarily like being touched and seems to be noise sensitive, jumping at the slightest high-pitched sound. These animals mostly inhale their food, and as a result, they tend to burp or pass gas. In chronic conditions, I dose may be helpful to change the cycle or the bile flow.

In acute situations, Nux vomica can also be used. Give I dose every 20 minutes, 3 times. After the first hour, you may repeat it twice more during that day and the next until the animal feels better. If there is no response, try a different remedy or seek professional help.

Ipecacuanha (Ipecac root) in the 6th to 30th potency is especially helpful if there is marked nausea that is also associated with respiratory problems such as coughing or asthma. You may notice the nausea as lip smacking, repeated or uncomfortable swallowing, or when the animal goes to the food bowl, looks at the food, and then leaves. The animal is not thirsty.

In acute situations, usually I or 2 doses is all that is necessary.

Arsenicum album in the 12th to 30th potency is the remedy for the "scaredy-cat" type. These animals may have diarrhea and vomiting closely following one

another. It is a major remedy for *garbage-itis*, especially if there is any blood-tinged mucus in the vomit or stool. These animals feel very cold and like to sit on heaters or burrow under covers to keep warm. They seem weak when they are ill, and may either be thirsty for small sips frequently or not thirsty at all. They are very restless even though they are weak.

In acute situations, 1 dose every half-hour for 3 doses usually helps the animal feel better. You may repeat the remedy twice more during that and the following day.

WARTS

Warts are common in animals, either as puppies or kittens or when they grow older. Warts are benign growths that come on suddenly and sometimes bleed when the animal bumps it or bothers it. If the wart is bothering the animal, it should be checked by your veterinarian, because it may be an indication of a deeper problem. If it is just unsightly and bothers you, you may wish to try natural remedies. Homeopathy and herbs are effective in managing warts.

— *Homeopathy:* Both topical application as an ointment, and internally, **Thuja occidentalis** in the tincture form to the 30th potency is the most famous and successful treatment for warts. The warts may appear within one month following vaccination. The animals who respond best to Thuja will have warts on the inside of the cheek or on the paws. These warts are not bothersome to the animal.

WARTS, cont'd.

Use the lower potencies once daily for 10 days. Wait for another week to see if there is a response. Alternatively, you may use 2 doses of Thuja 30c spaced 12 hours apart, and then wait 10 days for a response.

Topically, the ointment should be applied twice daily.

Causticum in the 3rd to 12th potency is helpful for the animal plagued by warts around the lips, on the face, or on the tips of the digits of the paw. These warts will bleed easily, or be of the "horny" type attached to the paw pads. There may be discomfort when you touch them. These animals tend to have dry and possibly itchy skin, chronic ear wax buildup, and a history of back or neck problems. The toenails may be thick or misshaped.

Use 1 dose of the remedy for 3 days in a row, and wait 2 weeks to evaluate your response.

— _Topicals:_ **Milkweed, Dandelion,** or **Prickly poppy sap** applied fresh from the plant daily helps to eliminate warts.

— _Herbs:_ As warts are sometimes considered viral in origin, using an herb such as **Echinacea** to stimulate the immune system may be helpful. Give the liquid extract diluted at 35 drops to 1 ounce distilled water, using ½–1 teaspoon, 3 times daily, depending upon the size of your animal, for 14 days.

WEIGHT GAIN (see also _Hypothyroidism_)

There might be a glandular disorder occurring when your animal gains weight. Sometimes _you_ are responsible for the weight gain and are feeding the animal way

too much for the exercise that the animal is doing.

— *Diet:* Add fiber and whole foods to the diet. Many of the "light" diets offered commercially add fiber to the food, but this fiber may not be in a balanced form. Instead of the light diet, try adding well-cooked brown rice to the food and cutting back on the regular food. Add ½ cup rice and decrease the regular diet by ¼–½ cup. Alternatively, crumble a rice cake in with the food to add fiber and crunch.

Other forms of fiber are lentils, peas, and kidney beans—all of which can be added in moderation to the diet.

Psyllium husks can be added to the food to increase fiber.

— *Herbs:* **Dandelion** and **Milk thistle roots** help detoxify the liver and encourage intestinal motility. Use ¼–⅔ teaspoon dried herbs once daily for liver health and for invigorating the metabolism.

Ganoderma mushrooms and combinations: These medicinal mushrooms from China are available in tablet form in most health food stores. They increase stamina and may be used to help boost thyroid metabolism. Use ¼–½ the human recommended dose.

Kelp and other **Seaweeds** include trace minerals to help boost thyroid metabolism. Use ¼–¾ teaspoon daily depending upon your animal's size.

Lecithin granules are helpful to keep the circulation free-flowing and decrease plaque buildup in the arteries. Overweight animals will have sluggish circulation, making them more prone to heart or blood pressure problems.

Use ½–2 teaspoons daily depending upon your animal's size.

WEIGHT GAIN, cont'd.

— *Lifestyle:* Exercise plays a major role here to keep the metabolism up. Also, extra weight puts a strain on the back, hind legs, and heart. Take your dogs for regular walks and allow them to run free and socialize. For cats, make up games to pique their interest, and "play" with them. Play "feather, string, or toy mouse."

Sometimes feeding smaller amounts more frequently will allow your animals to regulate their own metabolism.

WEIGHT LOSS

Some animals live to eat, and some couldn't care less and would rather play. If, however, your animal is one of those who *is* eating and *is* losing weight, there may be an underlying problem with poor absorption or organ involvement, so please seek veterinary care. If your animal has lost appetite, this too may point to an internal organ problem.

— *Appetite stimulants:* If your animal is simply not hungry, it may indicate that the food is creating pain, gas, or acid burning. Experiment with the diet. Add some fresh foods, even some sprouts. Your animal may enjoy it. Otherwise, pour some natural vegetable or miso broth over the food as an enticement. Fresh meat seems always to stimulate the appetite, especially for cats.

— *Herbs* that stimulate the appetite are considered Qi tonics. They increase energy and absorption. Other herbs settle the stomach in order to pick up sluggish digestion.

Astragalus is a Chinese herb that is now cultivated in the States to improve the appetite, energy level, and enhance the immune system. Use liquid extracts in glycerine form, giving 10–20 drops on a crouton to stimulate the appetite.

Chamomile is helpful to settle the stomach of high-strung animals who would rather play. Make a strong cup of tea and give 1–3 teaspoons twice daily before mealtime, or a half-hour after dinner.

Wood betony is helpful for the nervous animal who is plagued with looking over its shoulder during eating. These animals will have sluggish digestion and will often vomit undigested-looking food several hours after it is eaten. This sluggish gut will decrease the desire for eating. Wood betony helps communication between the stomach and the liver, smoothing the stomach and intestinal contractions. Use the tincture, mixing 15 drops with 1 ounce distilled water, and giving $\frac{1}{2}$–$1\frac{1}{2}$ teaspoons once to twice daily between meals.

Swedish bitters are used to enhance the appetite. Gentian is one of its ingredients, and the bitter taste puts most animals off. Thus, it is best to give it in tablet or capsule form, using $\frac{1}{3}$ the human recommended dose.

Acidophilus combinations can increase the gut "good guys" and balance pH to help stimulate the appetite.

— *Lifestyle:* Encourage exercise to stimulate the appetite, and give the animal a relaxing atmosphere while eating.

WORMS

Parasites can plague all animals. Veterinary worming medications are effective, but sometimes harsh on the system, overworking the liver and leaving toxic residues.

It is easier to get rid of roundworms than tapeworms using natural means, as the tapeworm attaches to the inside wall of the intestine. Also, fleas carry the tapeworm eggs inside them, so whenever there are fleas, tapeworms may flourish.

— *Diet:* Controlling the amount of fats and sugar in the diet helps to reduce the food items that worms thrive on. Some doctors recommend a diet of boiled fish and oats to weaken worms.

Garlic has natural sulphur in it that helps repel fleas and acts against roundworms. Adding 1–2 cloves daily into the food is beneficial. If, however, your animal tends to get dry red eyes, garlic might make this situation worse.

Cabbage is also helpful for its sulphur-containing properties and does not redden the eyes.

Pumpkin seeds help weaken worm infestations. Use $1/2$–1 teaspoon every other day for 3 weeks mixed in with the food.

— *Herbs:* **Wormwood,** a relative of Mugwort and sage, is helpful in roundworm infestation. It is a very bitter herb that increases intestinal and uterine motility, so it must not be used in pregnant or nursing animals. Use the tincture, mixing 9 drops to 1 ounce of water, giving $1/2$–$1\,1/2$ teaspoons once daily for up to 14 days. Because of its bitter quality, some animals may foam at the mouth when you give it to them.

Alternatively, tablets or capsules may be used.

— *Health tip:* Animals with healthy immune systems and proper absorption are not plagued by chronic worm infestations. If your animal tends to get worms frequently, work on strengthening the immune system with acupressure, performance herbs such as **Astragalus, Oats,** or **Alfalfa**, or lymphatic drainage herbs such as **Echinacea.**

YAWNING

Yawning is a natural phenomenon, but some animals do it to excess. If your animals yawn quite frequently, especially when they change position or after they stretch the front legs out in a "bow" position, this may indicate an energy blockage behind the diaphragm and shoulder blade areas. The blockage may be part of a back problem or reflect liver congestion. The stretch-and-yawn is a type of self-chiropractic adjustment.

— *Massage* along the midline of your animal's chest and belly, in a downward and then circular motion. Then use circular motions to massage along both sides of the spine. This will help release tension and relieve liver congestion.

— *Massage* the inside of the hind paws, first in an upward sweep, and then downward. This will enhance the circulation and relieve liver congestion.

— *Nutritional:* Adding ¼–1 tablespoon olive oil every other day helps ensure gall bladder health. Feeding pieces of apple with the skin intact also fortifies liver functions.

YAWNING, cont'd.

— *Herbs:* **Burdock, Dandelion,** and **Milk thistle** help relieve liver congestion and free up circulation. Use ¼ teaspoon each of the dried herbs, making a tea in 1 pint of water. Steep for 20 minutes, strain, cool, and add 1 tablespoon of the mixture once daily to the food.

❖❖❖ ❖❖❖

APPENDIX

Common and Scientific Plant Names

Alfalfa	*Medicago sativa*
Aniseed	*Pimpinella anisum*
Astragalus	*Astragalus membranaceous (Huangqi)*
Bergamot	*Citrus aurantium*
Burdock	*Arctium lappa*
Caraway seeds	*Carum carvi*
Cardamom seeds	*Elettaria cardamomum*
Chamomile	*Chamaemelum nobile, Matrica chamomilla*
Chickweed	*Stellaria media*
Chrysanthemum	*Chrysanthemum leucanthemum*
Cleavers	*Gallium aparine*
Codonopsis	*Codonopsis pilosula (Dangshen)*
Coltsfoot	*Tussilago farfara*
Cumin	*Cumimum cyminum*
Dandelion	*Taraxacum officinale*

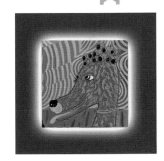

Dill	*Anethum graveolens*
Elecampane	*Inula helenium*
Eyebright	*Euprhasia officinalis*
Fennel	*Foeniculum vulgare*
Gentian	*Gentiana lutea*
Golden thread	*Coptidis*
Gravel root	*Eupatorium purpureum*
He shu wu	*Polygonum multiflorum*
Horehound, white	*Marrubium vulgare*
Horse chestnut	*Aesculus hippocastanum*
Horsetail	*Equisetum arvense*
Lady's mantle	*Alchemilla vulgaris*
Lavender	*Lavendula officinalis*
Licorice	*Glycyrrhiza glabra*
Lovage root	*Ligusticum levesticum*
Lycium (Wolfberry)	*Lycium barbarum (Gouqizi)*
Marigold	*Calendula officinalis*
Marjoram	*Majorana hortensis*
Marshmallow root	*Althaea officinalis*
Milk thistle	*Carduus marianus*
Milkweed	*Aesclepius speciosa*
Motherwort	*Leonurus cardiaca*

Mugwort	*Artemesia vulgaris*
Mullein	*Verbascum thapsus*
Myrrh	*Commiphora myrra*
Nettles	*Urtica dioica*
Oak bark	*Quercus alba*
Oats, Oatstraw	*Avena sativa*
Oregano	*Origanum vulgare*
Oregon grape root	*Berberris aquifolium*
Papaya leaf	*Carica*
Plantain	*Plantago major*
Prickly poppy	*Argemmone spp*
Red clover	*Trifolium pratense*
Red raspberry	*Rubus idaeus*
Red root	*Ceanothus*
Rehmannia—	
Chinese foxglove	*Rehmania glutinosa (Dihuang)*
Rose	*Rosa*
Sage	*Salvia officinalis*
St. John's wort	*Hypericum perforatum*
Saw palmetto	*Serenoa serrulata*
Schizandra	*Schisandra chinensis (Wuweizi)*
Shepherd's purse	*Capilla bursa pastoris*

Appendix

Siberian ginseng	*Eleutherococcus senticosus (Ciwujia)*
Slippery elm	*Ulmus fulva*
Spearmint	*Mentha viridis*
Tang kuei	*Angelica sinensis (Danggui)*
Teasel root	*Dipsacus silvestris*
Thyme	*Thymus vulgaris*
Wild cherry bark	*Prunus serotina, virginiana*
Wild yam	*Dioscorea villosa*
Wood betony (European)	*Stachys betonica*
Wormwood	*Artemesia absinthium*
Yarrow	*Achillea millefolium*
Yellow dock	*Rumex crispus*

❖❖❖ ❖❖❖

Resources

Associations and organizations

American Holistic Veterinary Medical Association
2214 Old Emmorton Rd.
Bel Air, MD 21015
(410) 569-0795

International Veterinary Acupuncture Society
P.O. Box 1478
1132 North Main St.
Longmont, CO 80502-1478
(303) 682-1167

Chi Institute of Chinese Medicine
9791 NW 160th St.
Reddick FL 32686
(352) 591-3165

Appendix

Academy of Veterinary Homeopathy
751 NE 168th St.
N. Miami Beach, FL 33162-2427
(305) 652-1590

British Institute of Veterinary Homeopathy
520 Washington Blvd., #423
Marina Del Rey, CA 90292
(800) 498-6323

International Association for Veterinary Homeopathy
334 Knollwood Ln.
Woodstock, GA 30188
(770) 516-5954

American Veterinary Chiropractic Association
623 Main St.
Hillsdale, IL 61257
(309) 658-2920

Rocky Mountain Holistic Veterinary Medical Association

311 S. Pennsylvania St.

Denver, CO 80209

(303) 733-2728

Institute for Traditional Medicine and Preventative Health Care

Portland, OR 97214

Flower essence products

The Flower Essence Society

P.O. Box 459

Nevada City, CA 95959

(800) 548-0075

AnafloraFlower Essence Therapy for Animals

P.O. Box 1056

Mt. Shasta, CA 96067

(916) 926-6424

Ellon Bach, USA., Inc.
644 Merrick Rd.
Lynbrook, NY 11563
(800) 433-7523

Western herbal products

Animal's Apawthecary
P.O. Box 212
Conner, MT 59827
(406) 821-4090

Tasha's Herbs
P.O. Box 9888
Jackson, WY 83002
(800) 315-0142

Frontier Cooperative Herbs
P.O. Box 299
Norway, IA 52318
(800) 786-1388

Herb Pharm

P.O. Box 116
Williams, OR 97544

Lotus Brands

Twin Lakes, WI 53181
(800) 684-4060

Halo

3438 East Lake Rd. #14
Palm Harbor, FL. 34685
(800) 426-4256

Homeopathic products

Boericke & Tafel

2381 Circadian Way
Santa Rosa, CA 95407
(800) 876-9505

Appendix

Boiron USA
6 Campus Blvd. Ste. A
Newtown Square, PA 19073
(800) BLU-TUBE

Dolisos America, Inc.
30014 Rigel Ave.
Las Vegas, NV 89102
(702) 871-7153

Hahneman Pharmacy
1940 4th St.
San Rafael, CA. 94901
(415) 451-6970

Standard Homeopathic Company
204-210 W. 131st St.
Los Angeles, CA 90061
(310) 321-4284

Arrowroot Standard Direct
83 East Lancaster Ave.
Paoli, PA 19301
(800) 234-8879

Homeopathic Educational Services
2124 Kittredge St.
Berkeley, CA 94704
(510) 649-0294

Dr. Goodpet Combinations
P.O. Box 4489
Inglewood, CA 90309
(800) 222-0032

Washington Homeopathic Pharmacy
4914 Del Ray Ave.
Bethesda, MD 20814
(800) 336-1695

❖❖❖　❖❖❖

About the Author

Cheryl Schwartz, D.V.M., graduated from Washington State Veterinary School in 1978 and has been practicing holistic natural veterinary medicine for more than 20 years. She is one of the original members of the American Holistic Veterinary Medical Association. Dr. Schwartz specializes in acupuncture, herbs, nutrition, and homeopathy, and is currently a veterinarian in the San Diego area. She teaches herbology, veterinary acupuncture accreditation courses worldwide, and is a frequent lecturer for humane societies and private animal training groups. Dr. Schwartz writes a holistic pet column for *Healthy Living* magazine, and is also the author of *Four Paws, Five Directions: A Guide to Chinese Medicine for Cats and Dogs* (Celestial Arts, Berkeley, CA 1996).

Selected Hay House Lifestyles Titles

Affirmation Cards

Miracle Cards, by Marianne Williamson
Wisdom Cards, by Louise L. Hay
Until Today Cards, by Iyanla Vanzant
Heart and Soul, by Sylvia Browne
Self-Care Cards, by Cheryl Richardson
If Life Is a Game, These Are the Rules,
    by Chérie Carter-Scott, Ph.D.
Inner Peace Cards, by Dr. Wayne W. Dyer
Power Thought Cards, by Louise L. Hay

Books

A Garden of Thoughts, by Louise L. Hay
Aromatherapy A–Z, by Connie Higley, Alan Higley, and Pat Leatham
Colors and Numbers, by Louise L. Hay
Dream Journal, by Leon Nacson

Healing with Herbs and Home Remedies A–Z, by Hanna Kroeger
Heal Your Body A–Z, by Louise L. Hay
Home Design with Feng Shui A–Z, by Terah Kathryn Collins
Homeopathy A–Z, by Dana Ullman, M.P.H.
Interpreting Dreams A–Z, by Leon Nacson
Natural Pregnancy A–Z, by Carolle Jean-Murat, M.D.
Pleasant Dreams, by Amy E. Dean
What Color Is Your Personality? by Carol Ritberger, Ph.D.
You Can Heal Your Life, by Louise L. Hay

❈❈❈ ❈❈❈

All of the above titles may be ordered by calling Hay House
at the numbers on the next page.

✳✳✳ ✳✳✳

We hope you enjoyed this Hay House Lifestyles book.
If you would like to receive a free catalog featuring additional
Hay House books and products, or if you would like information about the
Hay Foundation, please contact:

Hay House, Inc.
P.O. Box 5100
Carlsbad, CA 92018-5100
(760) 431-7695 or **(800) 654-5126**
(760) 431-6948 (fax) or **(800) 650-5115** (fax)
Please visit the Hay House Website at: **hayhouse.com**

Hay House Australia Pty Ltd.
P.O. Box 515
Brighton-Le-Sands, NSW 2216
phone: **1800 023 516**
e-mail: **info@hayhouse.com.au**

✳✳✳ ✳✳✳